SCHOLASTIC

Retelling Strategies to Improve Comprehension

Effective Hands-on Strategies for Fiction and Nonfiction That Help Students Remember and Understand What They Read

Darla Shaw, Ph.D.

New York • Toronto • London • Auckland • Sydney
Mexico City • New Delhi • Hong Kong • Buenos Aires

Teaching *Resources*

Acknowledgments

This book would not have been possible without the cooperative spirit, talents, and staying power of:

Peggy Stewart, Western Connecticut State University Photographer, whose photos appear throughout this book; Ellen Shea and her wonderful third-grade and fourth-grade students at South Street School in Danbury, Connecticut; Ben Shaw, my supportive husband, who gave me time and space for the project; Carol Ghiglieri, my supportive and understanding editor, who took me from research writing to a friendly venue; and Zella and Bob Hall, my parents, who encouraged me to be a lifelong learner with a willingness to take risks.

Cover design by Jimmy Sarfati
Interior design by Maria Lilja
Cover and interior photographs © Peggy Stewart, Western Connecticut State University

ISBN: 0-439-56035-7

2 3 4 5 6 7 8 9 10   40   11 10 09 08 07 06 05

Contents

CHAPTER 3
Retelling Extended: Vocabulary Development

Conclusion

References

Introduction

ॐ *What Is Retelling, Anyway?*

When I went to school I never learned about retelling. What is retelling, anyway?

As an educator, I hear this question a great deal, both from parents and beginning teachers. What, they wonder, is retelling, why is it so important, and how does it fit into the curriculum in our children's classrooms?

Quite simply, retelling consists of reading or listening to a piece of fiction or nonfiction and then orally reconstructing the key elements. With fiction, these elements are retold in order. With nonfiction, we ask students to retell in terms of structure or categories.

If you are already familiar with retelling, you may think of it as a strategy that's used exclusively with fiction. Retelling, for example, is often associated with picture walks through primary grade books. Increasingly, however, as much or more emphasis is being placed on retelling of nonfiction texts than fiction texts. And, in fact, researchers have found that retelling is beneficial to students at all grade levels. In the upper grades, retelling evolves into think-alouds with an emphasis on self-assessment, questioning, reflection, inferencing, and taking a critical stance. In other words, retelling is a skill that will benefit students for a lifetime.

There are a number of benefits to having students engage in oral reconstruction. When students retell something they've read, they are transforming a text into their own words, reflecting back only what is truly comprehended (Brown, Camborne, 1987). They are not, however, simply guessing at answers the way they might when responding to teacher-posed questions. Nor are they telling about a story "piecemeal." When retelling, students are using a holistic approach (Wittrocks, 1981).

Researchers have found that retelling is an interactive instructional strategy that helps students better process information, and therefore leads

The Comprehension Process

Student responds to reading with any prior knowledge on the subject.

Student previews material to get an overview of what is to be read.

Student forms one or more key focus questions for reading.

Student reads to answer the key focus questions with significant details.

Student retells the information that has been read, focusing on the key focus questions, related details, and critical reflections.

Student uses the retelling to monitor where he/she might need to go back and reread for more detailed information.

Student responds to open-ended discussion questions, test questions, or product application with information from retelling and rereading.

---

to enriched comprehension (Benson, Gambrell, Morrow, 1985). What's more, as students retell they can discover for themselves where they are having trouble and can then reread. They can also gain new insights into information as they hear themselves speak.

A Fix-It Strategy

In the classroom, the best teachers rarely if ever tell students the answers. Instead, they help students find the answers on their own. They have the students engage in "fix-it strategies" that allow students to solve their reading problems themselves. And when it comes to reading comprehension, there is no better fix-it strategy than retelling. Retelling makes students aware of their problem areas so that rereading, context clues, oral reading, and additional resources, including help from teachers or peers, can all be utilized (Marshall, Taylor, 1983).

Of course, retelling cannot be used as a fix-it strategy in isolation. Instead, I suggest using it as part of the total comprehension process I've outlined at left.

Ideally, as Shelly Harwin suggests, we want our students to reflect on the entire process, asking themselves questions such as:

- How did I go about getting the information?
- Was the process I used helpful or should I try something else next time?
- What will I do the next time I read a passage of a similar type to improve my comprehension skills?

Retelling as a Link to Critical Thinking

More and more in classrooms, we're seeing a move away from the types of exercises that ask students to circle, underline, or write in a one- or two-word answer. This shift reflects the understanding that these tasks fail to engage or strengthen processing skills or critical-thinking skills. In our efforts to help students build comprehension skills, we want to show them that constructing meaning is a process that includes accessing prior knowledge, making predictions, forming focus questions, retelling, reflecting, and connecting. Without retelling, students lose out on beneficial auditory reinforcement.

We now know that the teacher-focused questions that were once standard in most classrooms simply don't build students' critical-thinking skills. When students retell, however, they begin to integrate and personalize the content of what they are reading or listening to. Students begin to see how parts of the text interrelate and how they mesh with the students' own life experiences (Hartman and Allison, 1991).

Retelling is a generative task that requires the reader to construct a personal rendition of the text by making inferences based on the original text as well as prior knowledge (Kapinas, Koskinen, Marshall, Mitchell, 1986). When students are expected to integrate, use inferences, and make links to other venues, they are making full use of their critical thinking skills. Vicki Benson has developed a chart (see above right), which shows four crucial areas of critical thinking and how they relate to retelling.

The Link between Retelling and Comprehension

- **Process Thinking**
  Retelling requires knowing the who, what, where, when, why, and how and putting them together within the whole context.

- **Problem Solving and Analytical Thinking Skills**
  Retelling requires analyzing the story to determine what is important, then organizing that information for presentation in the retelling.

- **Language and Communication Skills**
  Retelling requires control of language in order to retell the story; retelling requires decontextualized language.

- **Independent Learner Skills**
  Retelling requires the student to define the boundaries; retelling is self-initiated.

Retelling Boosts Self-Confidence

Teachers have repeatedly found that students who are able to perform well-developed retellings generally score higher on activities requiring elements of creativity than students who have trouble with retelling. The ability to create language as one retells is helpful in problem solving and seeing a process through different lenses (Fieldstone, 1995).

The performance aspect of retelling can be intimidating to shy or quiet children. Creating a supportive classroom environment and allowing students to engage in "low-stakes" retellings (retelling to a stuffed animal, another student, their parents) will help build these students' confidence and abilities with retelling. The key to becoming a strong reteller is practice—and more practice.

Let me emphasize that for some students, retelling is not a necessary step toward increased comprehension. These students either internalize the retelling process automatically, retelling quietly to themselves, or they utilize other means to successfully master comprehension. I don't want to suggest that all children must retell in order to comprehend text, but rather that retelling is a useful tool for students to have in their toolbox. And even children who may not *need* to use retelling strategies may find that retelling deepens their comprehension or leads to other insights.

In short, I believe retelling has something to offer every student. Even those who may not need it as a comprehension tool may find that it gives them practice speaking in large and small groups. Many students, even the brightest, are shy and uncomfortable speaking in class. Yet we want our students to be at home sharing their voices and ideas, moving and speaking freely among their peers. Retelling offers even the shyest children a safe and supportive environment within which to speak and tell others what they know. It gives them practice in listening and speaking, and this practice helps build self-confidence.

> **"**When I retell, I hear my own voice say the information, not my teacher's voice.**"**
>
> —MAYA, FOURTH GRADE

A Tool in Students' Toolbox

Some of the retelling activities in this book are very simple, and some are more complex. But even the simplest retelling strategy will need to be modeled first at least once, and sometimes several times, before your students feel confident to venture out on their own.

As your students begin to engage in retelling and employ it on a regular basis, you'll discover that retelling can help bridge the gap between text and the construction of meaning. Retelling therefore becomes an essential tool in your students' toolbox, a tool that students need not use on a daily basis. However, they need to incorporate retelling when there are stumbling blocks in the reading and more clarification is needed. Retelling in some classrooms may take place only once or twice a week. As with any instructional strategy, teachers need to be aware of overkill. Variety is key.

Every student learns differently and some need retelling more than others. You should not force retelling on a student who already has strong comprehension and critical-thinking skills and has no need for this additional reinforcement. However, as I've already said, in many cases even our brightest students like retelling, as it helps to get them to new places in stories.

The following are a range of goals we can set for our students when retelling:

- Retell and add more reflection and insight to the story.

- Retell with more quotes.

- Retell and link to real-life experiences.

What Do Teachers Say About Retelling?

"Retelling gives the class a break from too much silent reading. It shows us where the problem spots are in the reading."

"I like retelling for the shy child. Retelling forces this child to be more interactive. If students have done the reading carefully, they will have something to say."

"Writing and retelling work well together. When children hear their words, it is easier for them to record them. There is more detail in the writing after a retelling."

"Retelling has become a regular part of my shared reading program. I read a story out loud. Then different students retell the story in parts. The next day one child retells the entire story. We then work on related story activities. I get many raised hands when I ask for someone to retell yesterday's story, especially if props are available."

"I am trying to get away from workbooks. Retelling gets me away from workbooks and into the writing process."

- Retell and link to other stories.

- Retell in greater detail.

- Retell and include more inferential anecdotes.

- Retell to find problem areas in the story.

- Retell to focus on comparisons.

Practiced retelling sessions can take many venues. The greater the variety of retell settings, the better the students will become at adapting their retelling for different populations and situations. Using different props can also help students visualize new ways to approach their retelling.

Venues for Retelling Practice Sessions

- In learning centers or stations

- Along with a computerized graphic presentation

- At home as part of a homework assignment

- Online with an e-pal

- With another class on the same grade level

- With children in a younger grade level

- With parents during a classroom visit

- With stuffed animals or dolls brought from home

- With people in the community on special community days

- With senior citizens who come to visit the school

The Role of Props in Retelling

Morrow in 1993 was one of the first researchers to suggest the use of props for retelling. He found that reconstructing stories by using props helped students build their memory skills and self-confidence levels. Fieldstone, another researcher in favor of props, has suggested that after teacher demonstrations, props be used by the students for practiced retellings, peer discussion, and role-playing. He also recommends keeping the props in learning centers so that students can choose to work with them independently.

Retelling can serve as a scaffold as it helps to bring a structure to either the fiction or nonfiction reading. Through prop retelling, students begin to visualize the proper chronology, the link to a variety of ideas and situations, and the emotional backdrop of the piece. Both the teller and the listener benefit from properly utilized props (Craik, Watkins, 1998).

Retelling Is Flexible

So what does a retelling session in the classroom look like? As I've suggested, there are any number of possible venues for retelling, from retelling to a partner to retelling to a large group, from three-minute retellings to retellings that run much longer, from individual retellings to group retellings. Our aim is to give students practice with retelling in whatever setting is appropriate and makes sense, so that they become comfortable with this comprehension tool. My aim in this book is to give you a number of strategies to implement with your students.

Retelling with props can be a quick activity or a more elaborate one. You will decide how much time and energy to give to the activity, depending on the needs of your students. And, of course, retelling does not have to be done with every book your students read, even in the primary grades. It's more important for students to develop the understanding themselves of when they need to implement retelling as a fix-it strategy. For this reason, some students in your class may be using retelling much more than others. In

" *I like to retell when I have a puppet, or a mobile or something in my hands. It helps me to remember and not feel so scared.* **"**

—KIM,
THIRD GRADE

order to conserve time, retelling is not always done in front of the entire class by one person. It can be done in a number of different ways:

- with a retelling partner

- in a small group

- as a round-robin activity

- as an interactive activity with the teacher

- into a tape recorder or video camera

Keep in mind that with longer texts, it is not necessary to retell the entire story. If students are having difficulty with a particular section of the reading, utilize only that portion for your retelling. Again, retelling is often employed as fix-it strategy and students needn't use it once the problem has been fixed.

The Application Phase

Retelling is a strategy that students can use in any number of situations, and one that they will, in some form, continue to use long after they leave your classroom. Many adults still retell, quietly to themselves, without even recognizing that they're doing so. Retelling is a way to take hold of information, and its usefulness does not fade.

But although this book is all about retelling, it's helpful to keep in mind that retelling is simply a tool to achieve greater comprehension. Mastering text is, after all, the ultimate goal, and in many situations the retelling will not be the final stage in the process. Often, students' retelling will be put to use in an application phase. We want our students to make use of the information they've read. We want them not only to be able to retell, but to use the retelling as a springboard for extended learning. They might:

- link their retelling of one story to the retelling of a similar story, then compare and contrast the two.

- link the retelling to a piece of related artwork.

- share the retelling with others.

- link the retelling to a written piece or simulation activity.

Application: Writing

While you may sometimes wish to have retellings function as an end in themselves, your students' retellings will often serve as an intermediary step. Once a student has taken the time and effort to focus, organize, and provide supporting information in a retelling, he or she is probably ready to take the comprehension to the next most logical step—a writing or application project. The retelling does not have to be followed by a writing or simulation activity, of course, and will depend on students' individual development. Some students may simply retell; others who are ready will go one step further, incorporating into a culminating project what they have retold.

When teachers are working with emerging writers, they often first take dictation from the student. Retelling is similar to giving dictation. Students put their ideas into their own words, words they feel comfortable with. Retelling functions very much like a prewriting exercise—an early step in the writing process. With a completed retelling, a student can more easily begin to plan a summary or reader response. The setting, characters, problem/conflict, attempts at resolution, and conclusion components have already been established. Students can easily transfer these elements to any number of possible writing formats. Below I show the link between a story grammar retelling and a straightforward book report:

- The introductory paragraph introduces the setting and main character.

- The next paragraph(s) gives more information (details) about characters and the problem at hand.

- The following paragraph(s) add more information about the main problem.

> **"**When I retell I sometimes get TV pictures in my head.**"**
>
> —MICHAEL, SECOND GRADE

- The next paragraph(s) focuses on the character's attempts to resolve the problem.

- The following paragraph(s) describes the result of these attempts and how the story concludes.

- The concluding paragraph(s) addresses the message, meaning, or insights from the story.

Story elements, grammar, and mapping are as critical to the writing process as they are to the construction of meaning in reading. With even the easiest picture books, students can write a basic five-paragraph essay using the story element format given above. For more complex stories, students can amend the structure. If there are several areas of conflict, numerous attempts at resolution, and several messages in a story, students can expand accordingly. We don't want students to think that there are always only two main characters, one problem, two or three attempts at resolution, and only one message in a story. We want them to understand that writing can be and often is complex and varied.

When going from retelling to writing, students have many options. The simplest, of course, would be to write a summary based on their retelling. Some of the other possibilities that can come from fiction retelling are:

- a compare-and-contrast paragraph or essay, using a similar story;

- a rewriting of the story as seen through the eyes of a major character in the story;

- a paragraph or essay based on an open-ended reader response question posed by the teacher or the student;

- an alternative ending for the final retelling;

- a paragraph or essay based on a key word or quote from the retelling;

- a descriptive essay based on a particular story element;

- an essay on whether or not the main character was correct in his or her choices; and

- an open-ended reader response entry.

Some of the products that can come from a nonfiction retelling are:

- a compare-and-contrast essay on people or places in history;

- a detailed time line on a historical event;

- a process chart on the production of an item;

- a science or social studies paragraph or essay based on a mini-fact-book retelling;

- a dramatization of an event based on the retelling;

- a persuasive paragraph or essay writing based on the pros and cons covered in the retelling; and

- a newscast, a press conference, or a mock interview with information gathered and used in the retelling.

Writing is a natural follow-up to retelling, allowing the student to extend the material he or she has just mastered. The writing doesn't necessarily have to follow the retelling in format. In fact, it's good when the writing takes on different forms, based on information from the retelling instead of simply replicating the retelling itself. As mentioned above, you will decide, based on what is developmentally appropriate for each student, when to move from retelling to the writing stage. However, even if students aren't developmentally ready to link the retelling with writing, they will see models of it being done in the classroom. What's more, reading, writing, and retelling are interconnected activities. As students become better retellers there is naturally improvement in the processing skills for both reading and writing, and vice versa. By using this reading/retelling/writing cycle regularly, students are building on their visual, auditory, and tactile abilities in a unique combination.

Application: Simulations

Simulations take a real-life situation and turn it into an activity or role play. One appeal of these activities is their ability to demonstrate real-world application. They can also motivate students to work together in pursuit of common goals and to apply the knowledge they've gained through reading, retelling, and, in some cases, writing. The interactive component and critical-thinking elements of simulations make them indispensable in the classroom.

Simulations are usually worked on in groups. This cooperative aspect lends these activities a rich component. Students must be able to work both as an individual and as a group learner. It's important to make sure with such group projects, however, that stronger, more dominant students don't take over for the shyer or less able ones.

Simulations can be time consuming, but the hours involved in the processing and development are well spent. Simulation exercises involve myriad skills, multiple intelligences, and are multisensory. As mentioned above, they also include cooperative learning, adherence to rubrics, reflection, and self-assessment. You can tell from simulation exercises how well students have comprehended and mastered ideas in the material. With a simulation exercise students apply what they have learned, rather than simply parroting back the answers.

Listed below are ten well-developed application exercises that can involve individuals or small groups of students. Each activity is open-ended in nature and can be modified in numerous ways. All of the simulations are challenging and involve high levels of critical thinking. In some cases, the students with less ability take a less challenging part in the project. They can become reflective listeners when the application exercise is shared. A reflective listener is one who must give supported feedback on the presentation.

1.) **Mock Trials:** Following a problem-related reading and retelling, students decide to put a particular character or person on trial. Some students serve as jurors, while the more active retellers act as the witnesses and the lawyers. The trial may be scripted or ad-libbed with note-card prompts.

2.) **Mock Interviews:** After reading and retelling a work of fiction or nonfiction, students put on a panel discussion or a one-on-one interview similar to what they might see on a television interview program. The moderator asks questions and students, taking on the role of different characters—or real people, if the source material is nonfiction—answer the questions based on their understanding of the characters they are portraying. The students can have questions ahead of time to help them prepare for the interview.

3.) **Readers Theater:** The terrific next step after the retelling of a story or a news article is a summarization of the reading with a Readers Theater script. Students' script includes dialogue for one or more narrators as well as the major characters in the story or article. The script writing can be a cooperative venture or can be done by an individual student. Have students revise and edit the script before the practiced readings.

4.) **Press Conference:** For a retelling based on a key character or personality, students develop a press conference. This press conference is similar to a mock interview. However, in this case, the main character or personality is asked a variety of questions by the public and not just by the moderator. Ask students when they think a press conference might be more fitting than a mock trial.

5. **A Living Museum:** Nonfiction retelling transfers wonderfully to a living museum piece. For this activity, students decide on various aspects of the material that lend themselves to demonstration stations around the room. Each station involves an activity that is manned and explained by a knowledgeable student. For example, if students were enacting a living museum for Lewis and Clark, the following stations might be developed:

- a model of their boat

- a map of their trip

- an interactive time line of their trip

- a station focused on the Indians who assisted them in their adventure

- a station showing the food that they ate

6. **Book Sale:** Turning the retelling of a book or story into a book sale is an excellent simulation. Students pick the highlights from the retelling for an animated book sale. The purpose of this retelling would be to "sell" the story to other students so that they will want to read the book. This retelling omits the book's ending, so that the listener will have a purpose for reading.

7. **Literacy Circle:** The summarizer or reteller in a literacy circle plays a critical role in the comprehension process. Usually the reteller of the chapter goes first, so that students who are having difficulty with comprehension will better understand the story. Once students are able to act as summarizer/reteller they are ready to go on to be connectors, predictors, vocabulary people, and illustrators.

8. **Teacher of the Day:** When students become experts on a particular topic through research and retelling, they are allowed to be teacher for a class period. In the role of teacher, students retell their information to the class, but they do not read to them. The teacher of the day must also lead an active discussion following the reading, and/or get the students involved in an application/assessment piece.

9. **Characterizations:** Following a reading and retelling about a particular character, students create a monologue that demonstrates their comprehension regarding that person. Their goal is to make this person come alive. Having the students dress accordingly and capturing the characterization on videotape are further ideas.

10. **A Meeting Between Characters in Two Different Stories:** After retellings of several stories or articles, have students pair off. Within each pair, have one student choose a particular character or personality from one of the stories or articles. Have the other student select a character from a different piece of writing. Then have the two characters meet. Based on the students' knowledge of both of the characters' personalities and experiences, they develop a dialogue. This joint meeting simulation works best when characters have something in common, even if the two are from different places and time periods. For example, if Ramona from the Beverly Cleary books met Pippi Longstocking from the Astrid Lindgren books, what would they say to each other? What would the two talk about?

The links between retelling, writing, and simulation exercises are important and useful. It does not matter how many stories a student reads; what matters is the degree to which students are able to absorb, retain, and utilize what they've read.

In the pages to come, I will describe a number of teacher-tested retelling strategies to be used in your classroom in ways that best meet your students' needs. Remember, retelling is flexible and can be used in any number of ways:

- as a quick fix-it strategy;

- as a group activity that involves listening and shared retelling;

- as a strategy that enables students to "own" the material they've read;

- as a way for students to reveal what they have and have not understood;

- as a way to give students practice listening and speaking in front of the class; or

- as a bridge to the next phase of study.

Retelling is all this and more. I hope you will feel free to experiment with and innovate upon the activities you find here. Be creative and flexible, and have fun!

CHAPTER 1

Using Props to Retell With Fiction Texts

For centuries storytellers have been handing down information through retelling. These storytellers may have changed certain elements of their stories, but the fundamental components never changed. Similarly, the comprehension-based retelling we use in our classrooms requires taking key elements from stories and then reflecting on the major elements.

Early storytellers used a wide range of props in their performances. It was not unusual for storytellers to use musical instruments, mime, simple costuming, or a variety of masks to aid them in their retelling. These props helped the storyteller to remember the various components of the story. The props also helped the listeners better remember what was told, because people often remember more distinctly what they see than what they hear.

Props are used every day in the classroom by teachers: flannel boards, story aprons, storyboards, flip charts, pocket charts, masks, puppets, and a variety of other items. Teachers use these materials effectively but rarely turn them over to the students for use in constructing meaning. You must certainly model for children how to use the props—but then students must have full access to the materials to practice on their own.

Most retelling props are easily found or made. You don't have to order them out of commercial catalogs. Some of the best props come from "found" materials, items that are no longer in use and that you can recycle for use in retelling. You might assemble a box of raw materials and put them in a center. All students will need to add is their imagination.

After you have modeled with the regular classroom props, allow students to design their own props with as many unique found materials as possible. They can look around the classroom, borrow items from other students, and use craft materials to make what they can't find. The more imagination they bring to the invention of props, the better. This in itself is a marvelous exercise in critical thinking.

In this chapter, I've divided the props into four categories, and as you will see, each category appeals to two or more senses:

- **Props Using Parts of the Body**
  (Senses used: visual, tactile, auditory)

- **Illustrative Props** (Senses used: visual, auditory)

- **Other Props** (Senses used: tactile, visual, auditory)

After materials have been produced, you may wish to box and label them so that students can access them whenever they need. The use of props works best when students choose their own technique for retelling, rather than being told exactly what to do. We want students to make their own connections to props and then be able to support their choice.

Retelling props are like a security blanket for beginning readers. Some students need props for a year of two. Other students feel free retelling without any aids right away. When students no longer need to do worksheets because they have mastered a skill, we stop using them. When students no longer need graphic organizers because the structure is internalized, we put them away. The same is true for retelling props, unless the student is using them in a creative manner. Workbook pages, graphic organizers, and retelling props are all aids to get us where we need to go. Once we get to our destination and no longer need the assistance of a prop, the props are dropped. In the outside world the students will not have access to manipulatives and props. They need instead to be self-sufficient and turn to the skills that have been internalized through use of these props.

Third-grade students display their retelling vests.

Retelling Using Parts of the Body

The simplest and most readily available props of all are found on students' own bodies. We have long been having students use their fingers to perform a number of functions in the classroom. Fingers used as manipulatives can provide a necessary visual-tactile comprehension link for learners. When students use movement along with parts of the body to demonstrate comprehension, they are processing the information in multiple ways, which helps the brain retain the material.

The following are some examples of finger exercises you may already be familiar with.

Manipulation of fingers . . .

- **to find out if a book is too hard to read:** Each time students find a word they can't read, they put down a finger. After five fingers on a page are down, they look for an easier book.

- **to learn to multiply:** For certain multiplication tables, a designated number of fingers are lowered and counted to get the correct answer.

- **to show correctness:** The teacher reads a statement. If the statement is correct the students put thumbs up. If the statement is incorrect, students put thumbs down.

- **to learn notes on the scale:** Students can practice easy songs on their fingers because each finger is assigned a different note.

In addition to being instantly accessible, fingers or other body parts are beneficial props because using them offers a dual mode of reinforcement—the visual and the tactile—and thus the student stands a greater chance of retaining the material. Even when the students may not be physically using their fingers any more, the repetition will in most cases have left an imprint in the mind.

Finger Retelling for Story Grammar

Whether you refer to this concept as story elements, story mapping, or story grammar, the idea is the same: identifying the five key elements that make up a story. These elements are

- setting,

- characters,

- problem (conflict),

- attempts at resolving the problem, and

- conclusion.

We want students to master these elements early on so that they will be able to comprehend fully the stories they'll read later. Understanding these elements also helps students write their own fictional stories.

USING THE STRATEGY

Finger retelling is a simple strategy that assists students in focusing on the story elements in their reading. In finger retelling, each finger is assigned one of the five key story elements. As students retell an element, they hold up one of their fingers, both as a prompt and as a way to register that a particular element has been covered in the retelling.

With older students, we might ask them additionally to identify the "message" or "moral" of the story. This sixth element can be incorporated into their retelling by having students circle the palm with a finger from their other hand as they retell this segment. As a quick and easy strategy, the visual/tactile/auditory aspects of finger retelling make it extremely helpful in getting students with differing learning styles to retell chronologically and in an organized story format.

Following is a sample lesson using finger retelling with the story *Strega Nona* by Tomie dePaola with a group of second graders.

DS: I want you to put your hand out with the palm down. You will see three or four major lines or veins running through the top of your hand. Can you touch these lines and give me three or four predictions about the story *Strega Nona* from the title and what you see on the cover of the book?

Try These Books

Amelia and Eleanor Go for a Ride
by Pam Muñoz Ryan

Amistad, a Long Road to Freedom
by Walter Dean Myers

The Great Kapok Tree
by Lynne Cherry

Sitti's Secrets
by Naomi Shibab Nye

Saint Valentine
by Robert Sabuda

Teammates
by Peter Golenbock

Tom: I see people dressed in old-time clothing so the story probably takes place in the past.

Claire: The people also don't look like people from America. I think the story takes place in a foreign land.

Ben: I don't know what "Strega Nona" means but it probably has something to do with the old lady who seems to be the main character.

DS: Good. Keep those ideas in mind. As we read the story, I want you to see if the predictions you made are correct. I already like the way you gave reasons for all the predictions that you made.

After we read the story together, I'm going to ask you to retell the major elements using the thumb for the setting, the index finger for the main characters, the middle finger as the problem/conflict finger, the ring finger for naming the attempts at resolving the conflict, and the pinkie finger for telling the conclusion.

[We read the story as a class.]

DS: Okay, everybody, hold up your thumb and let's talk about setting. Were Tom's and Claire's predictions right?

Jamal: (holding up thumb) They were both right. The story did take place a long time ago in a foreign land. It was Italy.

DS: Great. Now, hold up your index finger. What can you tell us about the characters?

Claire: (holding up index finger) The major characters in the story are Strega Nona, the good witch who helps everyone in the village, and Big Anthony, who is not known to be too wise or too trustworthy. He is left to watch over Strega Nona's house while she is away.

DS: Okay. And now the middle finger. What's the problem or conflict?

Lillian: (holding up middle finger) The conflict in the story comes when Strega Nona leaves Big Anthony alone with the pasta pot and he doesn't listen to her words about leaving the pot alone. To get pasta Big Anthony starts the pot and then he can't stop the pot from making the pasta.

DS: Very good. So now comes the fourth finger, the attempts to solve the problem.

Tom: (holding up ring finger) Big Anthony tries a bunch of things to stop the pasta pot. He tries magic words, he tries to give the pasta away, he tires to eat it all, but nothing works.

DS: Right. Okay, now let's wrap it up. The fifth finger is the conclusion.

Cheryl: (holding up the pinkie finger) In the end, Strega Nona arrives and stops the overflowing pot with her magic words. Then she punishes Big Anthony by making him spend the rest of his life eating the pasta he has made.

DS: Great job, everyone. You not only gave correct information for each story element, you gave support information as well.

The above lesson is one example of the many ways to use finger retelling with your students. In this case, the students are retelling in a whole group. You might also have one child retell the story to a group, to a partner, or directly to you in a retelling conference.

As mentioned above, finger retelling can be adapted for higher-level students by adding a sixth element—the message or moral. Students can circle the palm of one hand with a finger of the other. You can also ask students to make connections to other texts or to take a critical stance. Within the same class you might have students who are simply retelling while others are linking to critical thinking. This is what flexible grouping and individualization is all about.

Facial Retelling for Story Grammar

Facial retelling is similar to finger retelling (page 25), except the face is used instead of the hand. In facial retelling, a different part of the face signifies one of each of the five story elements. Some students prefer the tactile/visual response from the face as opposed to the fingers. Also, finger retelling works best when retelling to oneself or partner, but when a student is retelling to a group or the whole class, it is easier to see the facial retelling.

Try These Books

Froggy Goes to School
by Jonathan London

Harriet, You'll Drive Me Wild
by Mem Fox

I Like Me
by Nancy Carlson

Mean Soup
by Betsey Everitt

Stone Soup
by Jon J. Muth

Too Loud Lilly
by Sofia Laguna

USING THE STRATEGY

When doing facial retelling, students make their initial predictions as they touch or tap the top of the head.

- When students retell the setting (time/place) they touch the ears—one ear for time, the other for place.

- When students name the characters, they touch one eye and talk about one character and then touch the other eye to discuss another character. The eye is a meaningful choice because we usually see the story through the eyes of the key characters in the story. More advanced students might identify the characters in more detail and give inferred characteristics of these characters as they relate to the story line.

- When students name the problem, they touch the nose. The nose sticks out on the face the way the problem or conflict sticks out in the story.

- When students retell the attempts to resolve the problem, they can touch the front teeth.

- When students retell the conclusion, they circle the lips.

- Finally, if you wish to have students retell the message or theme of the story, have them cup their hand softly around their throat. This represents the area of speech and signifies what the story is "saying" and what it is important to remember.

As with finger retelling, facial retelling involves a variety of senses in the learning process, so students are better able to master the material.

Retelling Charades

In retelling charades, students act out the major events of a story, retelling through the use of the body and gestures. Here, we are not focusing on the five fundamental story elements of setting, characters, problem, attempts at solution, and conclusion. Rather, we are concerned with the major events of the story, the actual points of the plot.

USING THE STRATEGY

With the group, brainstorm the significant events in the story. Then, write them on slips of paper and place them in a hat, basket, or box. The number doesn't matter—if it's a small-group activity, everyone should be able to draw a slip of paper. If it's a large-group activity, it would be demonstrated using 10 to 12 different events in the story. Once the slips are drawn, have students act out the events, using only their bodies.

The following are the steps I follow with a group of third graders who are using retelling charades to retell "Goldilocks and the Three Bears."

1. I ask students to brainstorm a list of the significant events in the story in the order in which they take place.

2. Students come up with the following list:

> Goldilocks is walking through the woods and finds a cute house.
>
> Goldilocks walks into the house and finds no one home.
>
> Goldilocks sees chairs of three sizes. She sits in the small one and breaks it.
>
> Goldilocks goes into the kitchen and finds three bowls of porridge and eats one.
>
> Goldilocks goes upstairs to find three beds and she sleeps in the small one.
>
> The bears return home, and they find a broken chair.
>
> The bears find porridge eaten.
>
> The bears find Goldilocks asleep in the bed.
>
> Goldilocks runs out and never returns.

Try These Books

A Bad Case of Stripes
by David Shannon

No, David!
by David Shannon

Seven Blind Mice
by Ed Young

Sheila Rae, the Brave
by Kevin Henkes

Swimmy
by Leo Lionni

Tacky the Penguin
by Helen Lester

3. I write the events on a sheet of chart paper.

4. As we look over our list, I quickly write the events on slips of paper and put them in a basket.

5. I ask a student to circulate with the basket, so students can pick a slip of paper. Depending on the size of the group, everyone may not get to participate in the charades.

6. I instruct students to look at the event written on the slip of paper and to think how they will use only their body—no words or other props—to convey the event they've selected.

7. One by one, children act out the event they have chosen. We proceed around the room, starting with the student who picked first, and so on. Note that at this stage, we are not retelling in chronological order.

8. After each student performs his or her event, he or she stands in the proper sequential order. So, for example, the child who performs "The bears find Goldilocks asleep in the bed" stands in place *after* the child who performed "The bears find porridge eaten" and *before* the child who enacted "Goldilocks runs out and never returns." I remind students that we will be reshuffling the group continually as new people perform their retellings.

With more advanced students, you can use retelling charades to retell more sophisticated stories, and the retellings can take on a higher level of critical thinking. However, even a story like "Goldilocks" can go from a routine retelling to an insightful retelling with real sophistication. By using fractured or modified fairy-tale books with the class, for example, students will begin to see that folk- and fairy tales can be told in a variety of ways. With older students, a follow-up discussion can look at author's craft, story techniques, modifications to the stories, the focus audience, and many other elements.

These retelling strategies encompass a full range of complexity and difficulty. Students can be expected to retell only five or six key elements in a story using parts of the body as props. Students with more ability can be challenged to retell using inferences; actual quotes; character analysis;

and connection to other stories, the world, or themselves, without props at all. What's more, as standardized testing focuses on taking a critical stance and author's craft, these two elements can also be included in the retelling for the students who are developmentally ready. It isn't the age or grade of the child that determines how retelling is to be used; it is the prior knowledge, learning style, developmental level of the student, degree of self-confidence, and the student's willingness to take risks.

Retelling With Illustrative Props

Visual literacy is an integral part of language arts. In fact, after reading and writing, it shares equal footing with listening, speaking, and the use of technology. These days students are so bombarded and enticed by visuals that they need to know how to cope with them in a meaningful way. We want students to know that visuals are meaningful, and while they will never take the place of the written word, they can certainly enhance the information that is conveyed through print. For this reason, we want our students to acquire not only print literacy but visual literacy as well.

For years primary teachers have been taking their students on picture walks through books as a preview to reading. Their students gain a wealth of insight into the story with this technique. After a picture walk, students are better prepared to understand the story with the knowledge they have gained from the pictures.

Because of the impact visuals have on learning, it only makes sense that illustrations and related graphics would make beneficial retelling props. This chapter will demonstrate how illustrative props can become useful comprehension tools. Students enter into a dialogue with illustrative props, which provide another avenue for deepening comprehension. These props include retelling ropes, aprons, mobiles, mural stories, retelling vests, triaramas, and canned/boxed stories.

Retelling Ropes

Try These Books

Arthur's Teacher Moves In
by Marc Brown

Aunt Flossie's Hats
by Elizabeth Fitzgerald Howard

Click, Clack, Moo, Cows That Type
by Doreen Cronin

Five Little Monkeys with Nothing to Do
by Eileen Christelow

Miss Nelson Is Missing
by Harry Allard

Olivia
by Ian Falconer

Students use a retelling rope to retell the five story elements. You can buy retelling ropes at a teacher store or make your own to put in a center, or have students make retelling ropes themselves—as a whole-group or small-group activity, or individually at home. A retelling rope is a thick piece of rope with icons signifying the five story elements. Using this prop, with its visual and tactile stimuli, students can retell the elements of simple or complex stories.

MATERIALS
- length of rope (for each student) about a foot long, purchased at a hardware or general store
- magazines or clip art (selected ahead of time)
- scissors
- stapler

USING THE STRATEGY
To make the retelling rope, follow these instructions:

1. If you've already chosen images, distribute copies of them to students. I like to let older students have some say in the images they choose for their retelling ropes. For younger children, you might wish to choose the images for them. If you're using old magazines, give children time to comb through the pages to select one image for each of the story elements. Note that the images they're searching for will represent the five elements *in general*, and don't pertain to any particular story. For example, a clock might represent setting; a key might represent the story's solution, and so on.

2. Students select their five images and cut them out. When students select images themselves the images have greater meaning for them. The process also engages critical-thinking skills.

3. Have students staple their images along the length of the rope, at even intervals, making sure to put the icons in the order in which they will retell: setting, character, problem, attempts at resolution, conclusion. (More-advanced students might include a sixth image, signifying theme or meaning, which they can then include in their retelling.) You may wish to help younger students staple the pieces onto the rope. Alternatively, you may go around and fasten the icons with safety pins.

4. After students have read or listened to a story, they can use the retelling rope to retell the five key elements. In a whole-class setting, you might invite several students to retell after a read-aloud. Older students might retell to the class as they prepare to write a book review. Students can use the retelling rope to retell in small groups, with a partner, or directly to you. And as with many of the retelling strategies, they can use the retelling rope to retell to themselves, as a fix-it strategy.

This retelling rope uses small objects to represent story elements.

Retelling Aprons

A retelling apron is similar to a flannel board. With a retelling apron, the student retells the story, manipulating the various characters and key items in the story so they appear and disappear on the surface of the apron at the appropriate time. For this activity you can buy an inexpensive bib apron at a craft or discount store.

The retelling apron is a good strategy to use when you're working with a story that's relatively uncomplicated and that doesn't have too many characters. Children love to put on the retelling apron. It makes them feel special and in charge!

MATERIALS

- bib apron with pockets
- Velcro fasteners
- photocopied illustrations from the story or handmade illustrations

USING THE STRATEGY

Introduce apron retelling to your students, making sure to model for them how the key illustrative props help you with the retelling. Your props should be pictures of major characters in the story as well as any important objects or symbols. The idea is to use only the props that are essential to the retelling. Extraneous props can bog you down and impede the fluency of the retelling. Attach Velcro strips to the back of your illustrations as well

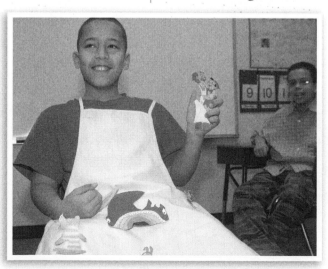

as to the apron, using these props as cues as you retell. Once the students have seen you model the story with the related props, they can begin to assist you. After this modeling activity, students will be ready to use the retelling apron on their own.

In advance of a student's retelling, he or she makes the needed props. It's up to you whether the student will use photocopies of illustrations from the book or create his or her own illustrations with craft materials. The student wearing the retelling apron keeps his or her props in the apron pockets or on a table, whichever the student prefers. Many students like having the props on a table, so they can lay the items out in the proper order prior to the retelling. Of course, the characters and some of the items will be used more than once in the retelling.

Students can also retell in pairs or small groups, depending on the number of retelling aprons you have. I've also seen teachers use this activity for individual retelling, wherein the student sits quietly at his or her desk and retells on his or her own, using the props at hand. This wonderful individualized study skill helps students reinforce story elements, the visualization process, and methods of linkage.

Moving Through a Mural

Like many of the retelling strategies in this section, Moving Through a Mural appeals to students who process information visually. With this activity, students create a mural that springs to life. Craft-stick "puppets" move through the mural as the students retell the major events of the story.

MATERIALS

- long sheet of butcher paper
- crayons, paint, markers
- craft sticks
- photocopied illustrations from the text or white construction paper for drawing props
- other craft materials (optional)

USING THE STRATEGY

There are many ways to use this activity in your classroom. With older children, you might assign different stories to different groups, have each group work on the project at the same time, and then have them each retell to the class. Or, you may wish to have one group retell a story the whole class has read. With younger students, you might want to make this a whole-class activity, as they will need more guidance from you. Feel free to use and adapt this and all strategies in this book in whatever way best suits the needs and practicalities of your classroom and schedule.

Try These Books

Grandfather's Journey
by Allen Say

Possum Magic
by Mem Fox

The Princess Knight
by Cornelia Funke

Strega Nona
by Tomie DePaola

Three Days on a River in a Red Canoe
by Vera B. Williams

The True Story of the 3 Little Pigs!
by Jon Scieszka

1. On the butcher paper, children use crayons, markers, or paint to create the backdrop or scenery for the events in the story. In the book *The Paper Bag Princess*, for example, the story begins at the castle, continues into the forest, arrives at a cave, goes to an open field, and ends on a road to the castle. Make sure students illustrate all the major settings in the story, and put them in the proper order.

2. Once all the scenery has been illustrated, have children cut a slit across the middle of the chart paper. Assist them if necessary.

3. Students make props representing the major characters and key objects in the story. For *The Paper Bag Princess*, for example, the main characters would be a dragon, a prince, and a princess. The main objects that also factor in the story are a cave, a burst of fire, a meatball, and a tennis racket for the prince. If you wish, you can photocopy illustrations from the book and hand out copies to students. Or, have students make the props themselves.

4. Students cut out figures and glue them to the craft stick to make puppets.

5. To perform the retelling, two students, one at each end, hold the mural at waist level in front of the audience. One or more students stand behind the mural and slide the puppets through the slit in the mural, "acting out" the story. Students position the figures through the slit so that the figures are visible to the audience. One or more other students orally retell the story. The oral retellers and the students moving the figures coordinate their retelling so that they are in concert.

Students display their craft-stick puppets.

This is one of the more performance-oriented retelling strategies—and it can have the feeling of putting on a show. There are many steps and it can become a well-rehearsed project. A few things to keep in mind:

- Have students determine the number of settings in advance and block the mural accordingly.

- Make sure the key story elements take place in the proper order. Getting chronological order is important here!

- As a variation, you can ask students to let each puppet tell the story through his or her own eyes.

- You can lead an interesting discussion once the retelling is complete. You might ask students if their retelling differed in any way from the original story, and if so, how.

- The number of panels in the mural and the number of props will, of course, vary from book to book. The students retelling the story make the decisions regarding the panels and props. With this retelling procedure the students are given true ownership of the product. This ownership will also help to bring comprehension mastery along with pride.

Illustrative Retelling Vests

Another fun and creative prop for retelling is an illustrative retelling vest. Students create vests from brown paper grocery store bags, then use paint, crayons, markers, glue, construction paper, magazine cutouts, and other craft materials to illustrate the story elements. Because a vest has three panels—two half panels in front and a large panel in back—you can arrange the five story elements into three sections when using retelling vests. On the left panel (the wearer's left), have children include illustrations of the story's setting and characters. On the back (and largest) panel, they illustrate both the conflict and the characters' attempts at resolving it. Finally, on the right panel they focus on the story resolution, conclusion, and, with more advanced students, the story's theme or message.

MATERIALS (for each vest)

- brown paper bag
- scissors
- glue
- crayons, markers, and other craft materials

USING THE STRATEGY

Have students make simple vests, and then decorate them as a way to retell the main elements of a story. To make retelling vests, have students follow these instructions:

1. Open the paper bag and cut an opening up the center of the front panel.

2. With the bottom of the bag facing up, cut an opening in bottom to create space for the head.

3. Cut arm openings in the sides of the bags. Younger students may need extra assistance.

Once these simple vests have been made, students can begin the more involved process of illustrating the story elements for their chosen texts. Once completed, students can put on their vests and perform their retelling in small groups, or for the whole class. When every student has completed a vest of his or her own for a different story, you may wish to invite another class or parents to a retelling parade.

VARIATION

You may also wish to make a "class" retelling vest, using an inexpensive fabric such as felt, cotton, or even plastic (such as a garbage bag). Students can take turns wearing the vest and using it to retell throughout the year. In preparation for retelling, they can make their own props ahead of time, back them with Velcro, and adhere them to the vest.

Try These Books

Amazing Grace
by Mary Hoffman

Chicken Sunday
by Patricia Palocco

The Faithful Friend
by Robert D. SanSouci

The Funny Little Woman
by Arlene Mosel

Teacher from the Black Lagoon
by Mike Thaler

Three Names
by Patricia MacLachlan

Triaramas

When we ask students to create their own representations of characters and settings from a story, we are asking them to demonstrate their comprehension. The details they include in their illustrations let us know how much of the text they have internalized, and we can read these products just as surely as we would read a workbook page or a test.

MATERIALS

- construction paper (precut into 10-by-10-inch squares)
- construction paper scraps
- glue
- scissors
- crayons, markers, and other craft materials

USING THE STRATEGY

Illustrative triaramas are three-dimensional, three-sided triangular displays. Children first make the display, then they use the finished triarama to retell the important parts of a story in small groups, to a partner, or to you in a retelling conference. Children can make the triaramas independently or with a partner. Three and four triaramas can be put together to form a multiscene, multisided display.

Try These Books

Cloudy With a Chance of Meatballs by Judi Barrett

Dogzilla by Dav Pilkey

Love You Forever by Robert Munch

Officer Buckle and Gloria by Peggy Rathmann

Owl Moon by Jane Yolen

The Graves Family by Patricia Palocco

To make each triarama, first model, and then have students follow these steps:

1. Take a construction-paper square and fold in half on the diagonal (upper left corner to bottom right). Press the crease and unfold.

2. Now fold on the opposite diagonal (upper right corner to bottom left). Press the crease and unfold.

3. Cut along the fold line from the bottom right corner to the center of the square.

4. Rotate the square as shown, and in the large upper triangle draw the setting or background from your story. (The two lower triangles will fold over each other and form the base of the pyramid.)

5. Fold up the two smaller triangles along the midline fold, overlapping them. Glue them in place. The triarama should now stand on its own.

6. To complete the scene, add characters and other objects to bring the illustrate important events from the story.

For retelling, I find it works best to have students make three or four triaramas and then glue or staple them together. Each section can be a retelling tableau for one major part of the story. So for example, in *The Paper Bag Princess*, one triarama would be decorated with a castle in the background, one would show a deep forest with a cave, another would depict an open plain, and the last one would show a road in the woods leading to the castle. And of course, important characters are added to the scene.

Canned/Boxed Retellings

Yet another way to engage students' imaginations and critical-thinking skills with illustrative retelling is through the use of a storyboard threaded through a cardboard box or a coffee can.

In this activity the student illustrates each major element in the story on a long, thin strip of paper that is threaded through a box or coffee can. As the student retells the story, he or she moves the strip of paper along to help illustrate the story's events. The activity lets students simulate a slide show or a movie.

With this activity, students not only show their comprehension through the retelling, they also demonstrate their level of comprehension through the original detailed illustrations they create. The slide show or chronological flow chart allows students to map the key events in the story. The illustrations trigger and assist the retelling.

MATERIALS

- retelling cans or boxes
- strips of white construction paper, 4 inches wide
- crayons or markers
- tape or glue

USING THE STRATEGY

I think it works well to have several retelling cans or boxes made up ahead of time and placed in a classroom center for use throughout the year. That way, students have only to make their "storyboards" and they're ready to go.

To make a retelling can, take a coffee can and cover it with plain paper. Then, with any sharp knife cut a 4-inch slit in one side of can. A box can also be used (any box roughly the same size as a coffee can).

Try These Books

If You Give a Moose a Muffin
by Laura Numeroff

Rapunzel
by Paul O. Zelinsky

The Little Engine That Could
by Watty Piper

The Mitten
by Jan Brett

We All Fall for Apples
by Emmi Herman

1. Have students take a piece of scrap paper and decide how many pictures they will need to retell the story and what should appear in each picture.

2. On a strip of paper, students section off the number of frames they need to retell the significant elements of the story. They can tape or glue paper strips to one another to create one long, continuous strip.

3. Students can then perform their story retellings with a partner or in front of the whole class, or in whatever venue you choose.

This activity works well when done with a partner for paired retelling. One person can tell half of the story while the other feeds the paper through the slit. Then the partners can switch roles.

For more advanced students, the canned retellings can also be a springboard for a compare-and-contrast analysis. For example, you might ask them to make links to previous retellings they have done. Or, you could use the activity to prompt an examination of key elements of the author's writing technique.

Retelling Mobiles

Try These Books

Aaron's Hair
by Robert Munch

Gingerbread Baby
by Jan Brett

I Heard Said the Bird
by Polly Berends

Jennie's Hat
by Ezra Jack Keats

Sadako
by Eleanor Coerr
and Ed Young

Tar Beach
by Faith Ringgold

In her research, Vicki Benson found that the linking of various story elements with geometric shapes was an important connection for association, recall, and retelling. Working from this insight, she assigned geometric figures to various story elements and shared these pairings with children. To setting and characters, she assigned a triangle. To the problem or conflict and the attempts to resolve it, she assigned the rectangle. And to the conclusion and the message, she assigned the circle. These shapes can be strung on a simple coat hanger to make a retelling mobile.

MATERIALS
- coat hangers
- string
- crayons, markers
- hole punch
- scissors

- glue
- three strands of string (of varying lengths) per mobile
- large triangles, rectangles, and circles cut from colored construction paper
- old magazines

USING THE STRATEGY

To make the retelling mobile, follow these instructions.

1. Have students work in pairs. Give each pair a hanger, three pieces of string, and one of each of the three shapes. (Shapes will have a hole at the top, which you have punched ahead of time.) Explain to students that the shapes are going to be used to represent different aspects of the story:

   - The triangle represents the setting and main characters. That's one side for the setting, and the other two sides for characters. (Be sure to choose for this activity stories that have no more than two main characters.)

   - The rectangle represents the problem or conflict, and the attempts to solve it. (If possible, choose stories in which there are three attempts to solve the problem.)

   - The circle represents the conclusion. (With older or more advanced students, you might wish to ask them to identify the theme of the story or have them make connections to others stories or to their own experience.)

2. Next, have student pairs select illustrations—pictures from old magazines, pictures they draw themselves, or some of each—and glue them to the geometric shapes.

3. Students thread a piece of string through the hole at the top of each shape and tie a knot. Then they tie the string to the hanger. As they do so, students retell to their partner. If there's time, you might have volunteers retell to the whole class. Mobiles can be hung on a clothesline in the classroom, or taken home for more retelling practice.

Although students' illustrations can be comprised of clip art, computer graphics, images from periodicals, or simple line drawings, having students construct their own illustrative props for retelling encourages them to think visually. By creating their own artistic renderings that fit into a structured retelling, students have a powerful way to help them retain what they've read.

Other Props for Retelling

Props for retelling can come from anywhere. They can be math manipulatives, holiday decorations, old-fashioned play activities, or parts from childhood games. In fact, with creativity and imagination, retelling props can be just about anything from a box of crayons to a telephone to a deck of playing cards. The underlying principle here is that the prop itself is not important—it is, after all, just a prop. To the student needing structure, however, the prop is a facilitator that gives him or her the freedom to retell with confidence.

Here is just one example: Bring in a small rubber ball or kush ball (a fuzzy rubber ball) to class to use as a basic retelling prop. Begin by retelling the first segment of the story and then throw the ball to a student. This student must retell the next major event in the story before throwing the ball to somebody else. Students love this activity, and they are immediately engaged. Because students never know when the ball might come to them, they are alert and active, both attentive to what others are saying as well as thinking about what should come next. With this activity the student must continually reassess where the story retelling is going and where he or she may fit into the pattern at any time.

I'm always pleased when I see students coming up with their own prop ideas. As teachers, we should take note of this and give these students praise. They are demonstrating initiative and critical thinking in action.

The following are more retelling props that other teachers and I have found useful with fictional stories. Use them with your students to broaden the range of retelling props you use in your classroom.

Tangrams

A tangram is an ancient Chinese puzzle consisting of seven pieces: five triangles, a square, and a rhomboid. The pieces can be arranged to form hundreds of different patterns and shapes, including a perfect square. Tangrams are commonly used as part of the math curriculum, but, as we'll see, you can also use them as a prop for retelling.

MATERIALS
- tangram pieces (see reproducible on page 47)

USING THE STRATEGY
There are a number of ways to use tangrams for retelling.

- Each piece can be linked to a different part of the story so that when retelling, the student can associate a story section with a tangram piece.

- Any number of tangrams can be put together to form an abstract scene from any portion of the story.

- For retelling purposes, each tangram piece can be assigned to a story element: setting, characters, problem, attempts to resolve the problem, and conclusion.

- Two students can pool tangram pieces so that together they will have more material to use for a joint retelling.

Try These Books

Antarctica
by Helen Cowcher

Giants in the Land
by Diana Appelebaum

The House I Live In
by Isadore Seltzer

My New York
by Kathy Jakobsen

Keep in mind that tangram pieces are just props, and things do not have to be a perfect fit. When a story has more than one conflict or problem, or numerous attempts at resolution, encourage students to modify their retelling prop. This flexibility is part of the critical thinking we want to cultivate by retelling with props. Remember, the bottom line with tangrams, as with all other props, is that they're simply facilitators that help students take the focus off themselves and any nervousness they might be feeling. Instead, the focus is on the structure provided by the props.

Here's how a third grader used tangram pieces to retell *The True Story of the 3 Little Pigs!* by Jon Scieszka:

> I'm using the large triangle for the wolf. This triangle looks like the wolf's big open mouth. Then I am using the square to remind me of the brick house that didn't get knocked over from all the wolf's blowing. This small triangle reminds me of the small cell that the wolf was put in once he was captured. Finally, I am using the rectangle to remind me of the box of sugar that the wolf wanted from each of the pigs. Without this sugar there would be no story. I don't need the other three pieces. I can retell the story with only four of the tangram pieces that I have already used.

Tangram Reproducible

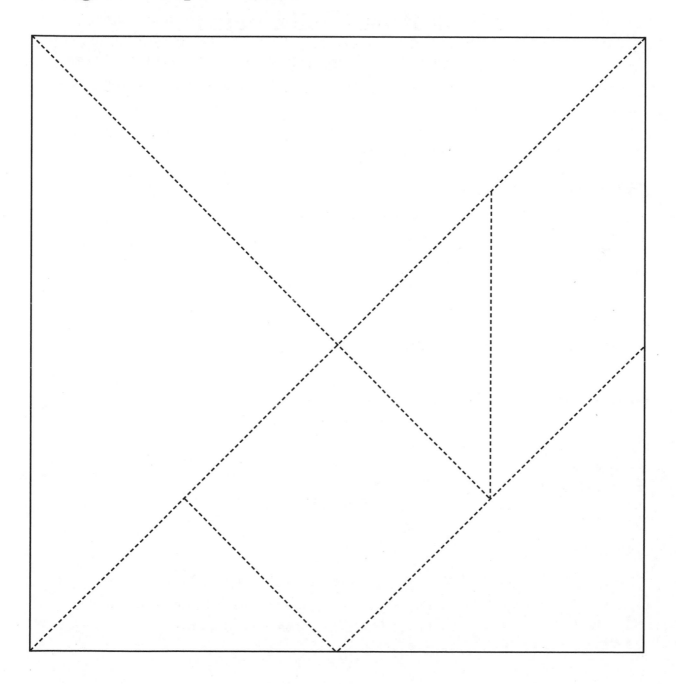

Character Retelling With Paper-Doll Chains

Children have been making paper-doll chains for generations. They enjoy tracing the pattern onto a folded sheet of paper and then cutting it out, making sure not to cut on the fold and thus disconnect all the dolls. We can use children's enthusiasm for creating these cut-out chains as a tool for a focused character retelling.

Try These Books

Baseball Saved Us
by Ken Mochizuki

Cinder Edna
by Ellen Jackson

*If You Traveled West
in a Covered Wagon*
by Ellen Levine

*My Rotten
Redheaded Older
Brother*
by Patricia Polacco

Smoky Night
by Eve Bunting

MATERIALS

- paper-doll reproducible (page 51)
- 11-by-17-inch sheets of white construction paper
- crayons or markers
- scissors
- other craft materials (optional)

USING THE STRATEGY

To make a single paper-doll chain have students follow the directions below:

1. Hand out paper-doll reproducible and have students cut out the doll.

2. Instruct students to accordion-fold an 11-by-17-inch sheet of paper 2 times (to create three panels).

3. Have them place the cutout on the top panel and trace.

4. Have students cut out the doll cutting through all three panels as they do so. Make sure that when children cut, the doll's left and right arms are not cut free, but are attached at the fold. (Be sure to model for students if they need guidance.)

5. For longer paper doll chains, tape or glue two chains of three together, to make six dolls in the chain.

There are many ways to use these paper-doll chains to focus on character. You might have students use an entire chain to focus on different aspects of a single character. So for example, in the story *Amazing Grace* by Mary Hoffman, several dolls in the chain could illustrate different facets of the character Grace. The first doll could show creativity; the second doll could show positive attitude; and the next doll could show enthusiasm.

Students could also use the dolls in the chain to illustrate different inner and outer characteristics. Or, you might have students draw a line down the center of each doll, with one side representing the inside, and the other side representing the outside. The dolls in the chain could show change or movement from one moment in the story to the next.

Another approach is to have each doll in the chain represent a different character in the story. Below is an example of a first grader retelling from a paper-doll chain. She's retelling from the book *When Sophie Gets Angry— Really, Really Angry . . .* by Molly Bang.

Tess: This first doll in the chain is Sophie. She is a little girl with yellow hair in pigtails and blue eyes. She gets really mad when people take things away from her. When Sophie gets mad she kicks, screams, and smashes things. Some people even say she is like a volcano exploding. But in the story she learns that when she gets angry she can not always be a volcano. She needs instead to go for a walk in the woods and listen to the birds and climb trees.

In the scenario above, Tess describes the character—her outward appearance and her inner characteristics. Then she tells about Sophie's problem and how Sophie attempts to resolve it. Finally, Tess shows us how Sophie changes in the story. Retelling about a character in a paper-doll chain encourage students to

- describe the character both inside and out.

- talk about the character's problem and how it is addressed.

- explain how the character changes in the story and how this change comes about.

The next character in the paper-doll chain might be Sophie's sister. The third character in the chain might be Sophie's mother, and so on. Students can retell in groups—with each child retelling about a different character—or in pairs, or individually.

One more variation is having students make life-size figures for retelling. They can do this by getting end rolls of newsprint or rolls of butcher paper, and then lying down and tracing one another's outline. After the life-size figures are cut out, the students can dress them to appear like the character in a story under discussion. In this case, the student may hold up the figure along with the retelling or attach it to a clothesline with clothes pins. The same key character elements would be used as with the paper-doll chains.

Third-grade girls display their decorated paper dolls—a variation on the paper-doll chain.

Paper Doll Reproducible

Rainbow Retelling Chains

Another perennial favorite with students is paper rainbow chains. These paper chains are made of different color paper strips that are interlocked and hung as decorations. You can use these colorful chains as a retelling prop to help students retell story events in chronological order. This is a good activity to introduce after a lesson on the main story events.

MATERIALS

- construction paper strips in various colors (1 inch by 11 inches)
- tape

USING THE STRATEGY

Here's how I introduced rainbow retelling chains to a small group of second graders. Before handing out the strips to students, I wrote different events from the story on the back of each one.

DS: We're going to make paper rainbow chains and use them for retelling. Each of you has a strip with a story element written on it from *The True Story of the 3 Little Pigs!* I want you to look at your slip of paper and try to remember as much as possible about that segment of the story as we all work together to give a retelling. Remember, we are only thinking about the *main* events of the story. Who thinks he has the first story event?

Neil: I do. I have "The Big Bad Wolf is going door to door for sugar." He wants to get sugar so he can bake a cake for his grandmother's birthday.

DS: Great. That is the first event in the story. Who thinks they're next?

Beth: I think I'm next because mine is "The Big Bad Wolf goes to the pig with a house of straw."

DS: You're right. Now, Beth and Neil, I want you to link your strips together to make a chain. Tape the ends so the strips interlock.

DS: Now we're ready for number three. Who thinks they have that slip of paper?

Ravi: I do. My slip says, "The wolf goes to the house of sticks."

DS: Hmm. Does anyone else have anything before the house of sticks?

Keesha: I do. I have the slip that says, "The wolf starts sneezing at the straw house and the power of his sneeze blows the house down."

DS: Okay, good, Keesha. That part does come next. Now add your strip to the chain.

Tiffany: I have the next one. Mine says "The straw house falls down on the first pig and kills him and the wolf eats him."

DS: Now we are back to the correct story order. Tiffany, add your strip to the chain, and we'll continue.

At the conclusion of the retelling, the chains can be hung from the ceiling or on the bulletin board. Or, an even better idea might be to disassemble the chain and leave the strips in a classroom center for students to practice with independently.

As older students become more proficient at independently retelling stories in chronological order, they can provide the written information on the strips. In fact, the sooner the teacher can turn over to students the task of writing, the better the chance for improved comprehension. When students write out phrases for other students to use, they have to make decisions on order, importance, completeness, and the significance of various elements of the text.

Artifact Boxes

One sure way to engage and motivate students is to introduce activities that involve boxes, bags, or other items that conceal. This quality of concealment makes the activity playful for students as they eagerly await to see what's inside. With artifact boxes, students themselves are the masters of concealment. They have filled their box or bag with special, meaningful items, and as they retell, they use these props to perform complete and elaborate retellings. This activity is fun for both the reteller and the listener.

MATERIALS
- shoebox or paper bag
- crayons, markers, pencils, and other craft materials
- various props associated with the story

USING THE STRATEGY

An artifact box is a shoebox or bag or any similar container. The outside of the container includes pictures or drawings related to the story. The inside usually includes five to ten props that help in retelling the story. Each prop can be a small item linked to the story. It can also be a drawing, a picture from a magazine, or a card with a word or phrase on it. In the classroom, students can search for props in designated prop boxes, or anywhere else they see something that would make a useful prop. Remind them to keep their eyes peeled! If students have several days to create the artifact box, they can also look for items at home. But remind them that what they can't find they can make. The real importance is in how the props relate to the retelling.

While younger students might select more literal props (a piece of spaghetti, for example, for *Strega Nona*), more advanced students enjoy using props that are less concrete and more symbolic and inferential. For example, in one retelling of "Cinderella," a student included a small perfume bottle. There is no perfume bottle in the Cinderella story, but it represented the sweetness of the character Cinderella.

Have students work with the artifact boxes following the directions below.

1. Choose a container (a box or bag brought from home, or supplied by the teacher) and decorate the container's outside. The decorations on the bag should be linked to the story in some way.

2. Locate between five and ten items to include in the artifact box. These items may be actual objects, original illustrations, cutouts from magazines, or words written on 3-by-5-inch cards. (Younger students can choose concrete, literal props; encourage more advanced students to think symbolically or associatively.)

3. Practice the retelling several times before retelling to a partner, a group, or the whole class.

This strategy can also be done as a group project. The box can be constructed and filled by the group, and then each member can retell a different part of the story, using a different prop.

To extend the activity, you might follow up the retelling by asking students to describe how they chose their props and why, and what they might do differently next time.

A variation of this activity is to have the reteller keep the name of the story a secret. Then as the student pulls out different props from the box or bag, he or she says nothing more than the name of the item. It is then up to the other students to determine the name of the story based on the "clue props" in the container. In this strategy, the whole class becomes involved and participates in the retelling.

Retelling can come after listening to a story. Retelling can come after reading a story silently. Retelling can come in parts or in a whole. It can be used for only a difficult part of the story or for a very dramatic story portion. Flexibility is the name of the game when it comes to retelling.

When students are exposed to a variety of props they begin to use their imagination. Additionally, the props have value because they "trigger" an association with what needs to be remembered in the story. They give students the structure and security to delve further into the key elements in the story. They also make learning more fun and we can always use more of that in a classroom.

In the next chapter, we'll look at ways to employ retelling with nonfiction texts.

CHAPTER 2

Using Props to Retell With Nonfiction Texts

I find that teachers generally feel more comfortable with fiction retelling than nonfiction retelling. This is understandable, since retelling got its start in the primary grades as a tool to use with picture books. In recent years, however, with the increased emphasis at all grade levels on expository reading and writing, nonfiction retelling has become a useful strategy with students of all ages and developmental levels.

Expository or nonfiction readings include textbooks, trade books, newspapers, other periodicals, brochures, and the Internet. With the exception of textbooks, these are categorized as "authentic reading materials." This means that all of these materials are found in the real world outside the classroom. Yet for everything from trade books to text books, retelling proves a useful comprehension tool. Research has shown that students who are able to retell nonfiction show improvement in oral language complexity, comprehension of story, and sense of story structure (Moss 1977, 1985, 1986).

In addition to using expository retelling with average students, retelling has been used with special needs students with a good deal of success. According to Gambrel et al. (1984), "The verbal reconstruction of the text helps the less-proficient reader as well as the more able reader to organize and to deploy their processing capacities more effectively." Retelling has also had a positive effect on the expository literacy skills of English Language Learner (ELL) students (Searfoss and Readence, 1994).

Students are often overwhelmed by the sheer volume of information they take in through reading and listening. As a result, they can't always decide what information is the most important to remember. All of the activities in this section are designed to help students "weed through" the volume of words and come away with the key elements in the text.

While fictional retelling focuses on story elements, proper chronology, and insightful reflections, expository retelling places an emphasis on categories of information, remembering important information, and ultimately being able to answer the following key questions:

1. How am I going to sort or organize this information? What are my category headings?

2. Which information that I am retelling is the most important? What do I need to remember most?

3. How can I further support the information in my retelling? Do I have details for all the important details I retold?

4. Can I make any connections between other topics/ideas and the information that I have just retold? Are there any connections to my life or to another story?

In this chapter, I will describe retelling activities students can use with the major text patterns:

- **Description** (by category)

- **Sequence**

- **Cause and Effect**

- **Problem and Solution**

- **Compare and Contrast**

- **Persuasion**

Understanding the text structure at work in a piece of nonfiction is a critical step in comprehending the piece as a whole. When students learn to recognize how a text is structured, they also learn to see what the text is doing—whether it's presenting a problem and offering solutions, demonstrating cause and effect, and so on. Understanding these structures will help students obtain a richer comprehension of the nonfiction texts they read.

With an understanding of the various expository patterns, students become better at retelling, too. In fact, students begin by linking the reading to a particular expository prop and then learn to retell within that structure. Learning is all about seeing patterns and using prior knowledge. With expository props and retelling, students learn how comprehension patterns can help them better understand a reading.

With expository retelling based on organizational patterns, students develop retellings based on one or more sources. These sources can include material from different readings as well as oral information from the teacher. Unlike fictional retellings, in nonfiction retellings several sources are often used to complete a well-rounded retelling, though this will of course depend on your curriculum and the level of individual students.

Props for Nonfiction Retelling

To get students involved in retelling from nonfiction sources, show them how to use props to structure what they have to say. Show them the props that link best to various comprehension patterns and let them choose the prop that works best for them. Keep reminding students that once they feel comfortable without a prop, they no longer need to make use of one. We want students to realize that in "real life" all they are going to have is themselves and the information and skills that are stored in the mind.

DESCRIPTION (by category)

- *Texts that use the description text structure give facts about the topic at hand, and then support them with significant details.*

The most commonly used nonfiction text pattern is description. Even though this pattern may seem easy for an adult to grasp, it can be extremely challenging for students. In order for students to fully understand the descriptive passages they encounter in textbooks and elsewhere, they must be able to pick out the most important elements and back them up with relevant details. The activities in this section—the Rotating Fact Wheel, the Eight-Page Mini Fact Book, and the Category Lantern—are all excellent props for helping students locate the main ideas and supporting details in the informational passages they read.

(Rotating Fact Wheel)

A fact wheel is a graphic organizer consisting of a large circle divided into six or eight pie-shaped segments (if more sections are needed, they can be subdivided). Each of these segments is labeled with a category heading for both note-taking and retelling.

MATERIALS (for each fact wheel)

- two 8 ½-by-11-inch sheets of oaktag
- pencils
- scissors
- ruler
- markers or pens
- oaktag circles (cut to the same size as the fact wheel)
- brass fastener

USING THE STRATEGY

Older students can make these fact wheels on their own. You will have to assist younger children.

As a group, have students brainstorm to determine the categories for the fact wheel before they read. For example, before a group of fourth graders read about the singer Marion Anderson, I gave a brief introduction, and together we brainstormed some topics or areas of focus for them to keep in mind as they read. Students came up with the following list of topics:

- fame (why was she famous?)
- education
- career background
- family
- when she was born and died
- problems/obstacles

I wrote the list on the chalkboard. Then students created their fact wheels, following the instructions below:

1. On one of the 8 1/2-by-11-inch sheets of oaktag, have children use a compass to draw a large circle with an 8-inch diameter. (For younger children, make a few oaktag templates ahead of time, and let children trace these onto their sheets of oaktag.)

2. Have students cut the circle out.

3. Ask students to divide the circle into six equal segments or pie pieces.

4. At the outer edge of each section, have students write one main idea or topic that you've brainstormed together. So, using the example above, students would write "fame," "education," "career background," "family", "when she was born and died," and "problems/obstacles"—one topic per section. If students can only come up with five categories, you can include the topic "miscellaneous" as the sixth. Tell students that as they read, they should be on the lookout for another topic that they will use to replace "miscellaneous."

5. As students read the article or passage, have them jot down words in each of the six sections (younger children can draw pictures). Encourage them to be as specific as possible, coming up with items that will serve as "triggers," helping them to elaborate during their retelling.

6. After students have read, ask them to draw and cut out a second, smaller circle (about 7 inches in diameter) on the remaining piece of oaktag.

7. Again have students divide the circle into six sections. This time, though, have them cut out one of the pie pieces. (Make sure they cut just one.)

8. Instruct students to attach the two circles with a brass fastener, with the smaller circle on top of the larger one. The cut-out pie piece should make a window, revealing one of the sections underneath.

The fact wheel can serve as a prompt when retelling independently, with a partner, or in a group. Students turn the top wheel to reveal key details that are important to remember. The fact wheel is also a fun way for students to study and assess what they know.

Eight-Page Mini Fact Book

Another way to gather main ideals and supporting details from descriptive texts is by using the Eight-Page Mini Fact Book. Students devote each page of the mini-book to a different main idea, and then fill in supporting information.

MATERIALS

- 8 ½-by-11-inch sheet of paper
- scissors
- markers
- pens, pencils

USING THE STRATEGY

First, model making the mini-book, then have students follow the directions below to create the mini-books themselves.

1.) Fold the sheet of paper in half widthwise. Fold it again, in the same direction.

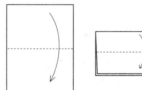

2.) Fold the paper in half again, but this time in the opposite direction.

3.) Unfold back to a half sheet. Beginning at the folded edge, cut along the crease. Stop where the fold lines meet.

4.) Open paper to a full sheet.

5. Fold the sheet lengthwise.

6. Holding the outer edges, push the ends toward the center, so that the opening balloons out. Push further until you form a book with eight pages.

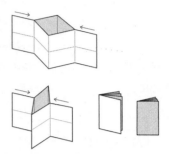

Completed mini-books can be used in numerous ways. As with the rotating fact wheel, younger students may use pictures in place of words. The category headings will be determined, of course, by the types of topics being covered. For example, if students were making a mini-book for soccer players, the page headings might be history, players, playing field, equipment, uniforms, famous players, and so on. If students were making a mini-book for Spain, the pages might be set aside for location/terrain, history, government, culture, religion, products, miscellaneous. For farm animals, the topics could be physical features, where on the farm the animal lives, what the animal is used for, size, and so on.

As with the fact wheel, the fact book categories must be brainstormed prior to the reading, so the students will know how to focus and organize their reading. And here, too, you can include a "miscellaneous" page that children will override later with their own discoveries. The fact book need not always follow the same format. The book can have a final reflection page, or a page for quotes, or anything else that has been a focus of class work. What makes mini-books such an excellent tool for retelling is their size. Their small size forces students to highlight only important information in key phases. They can also be kept in a pocket or bag for handy reference. Because the mini-books are small and portable, students can use them to retell anywhere.

Category Lantern

In this activity, students make a paper lantern that "sheds light" on the information in the text and the related retelling.

MATERIALS

- a sheet of 8 ½-by-11-inch paper
- pencil
- scissors
- tape
- scrap paper (from which to make a handle)

USING THE STRATEGY

Before the class reads the descriptive text, guide them in a brainstorming session to identify four main ideas or topics the reading will cover. Make a list on chart paper or the chalkboard. Then have students make a paper lantern, following the instructions below:

1. Fold a sheet of 8 ½-by 11-inch paper lengthwise. Fold again lengthwise.

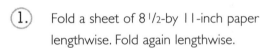

2. Unfold the sheet and refold widthwise.

3. Starting at the center fold, cut along the three creases, stopping within an inch of the edge.

4. Open sheet to full size and fold the two long edges together. Glue or tape in place.

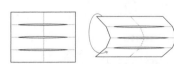

5. Add a strip of paper for a handle (see photo above).

Once students have made their lanterns, have them write one of the four main ideas on a strip of the lantern. (You may wish to have younger students draw pictures instead.) Then, have them write or draw related details under each flap. The lantern becomes a prop students can use to retell in whatever venue you choose.

Color-Coded/Symbol-Based Annotation

A more sophisticated strategy for category retelling is the color-coded/symbol-based annotation. For this activity, students need a copy of the reading on which they can write. They will use different-colored markers or pencils to differentiate main ideas, subtopics, and details.

MATERIALS
- photocopies of the textbook passage, news article, or other text being discussed
- makers or colored pencils

USING THE STRATEGY
Give students a copy of the text that they can freely mark up. As they read, ask them to mark up the text in the following way:

- main ideas: underline in red
- subtopics: underline in green
- supporting details: underline in blue
- unfamiliar vocabulary words: underline in brown

Depending on the level of your students, you may wish to do this as a whole-class activity or to let students work independently. As a variation, students can choose to annotate, using symbols instead of colors. So, main ideas might be boxed; subtopics could be enclosed in parentheses; details could be underlined; and new vocabulary words could be circled.

This strategy may prove challenging for students. Remind them that it will take a few repeated readings to unearth each of the categories. But the activity really pays off. With this technique, students can literally see a format emerge before their eyes, which they can then use as the basis for their retelling. They will see the main ideas as well as the subtopics they need to cover. The related details will fall into place after that. Unknown vocabulary words are easily singled out. Encourage them to add these to their word banks (see page 89) and include them in retelling.

Look at the following paragraph on fruit bats. You can see how the student has effectively utilized the symbolic approach even though the paragraph is not perfectly structured. Remember, instead of symbols the writer could have used a pattern of colors.

With color-coded/symbolic annotation, students can tell from looking at designated colors or symbols what they need to include in their retelling. They are gaining a sense of organization through visualization. When this is paired with an auditory retelling, the student is reinforcing not only the content but the patterning process. Annotation and retelling are key elements in gaining proficiency in both reading and writing.

> ## Fruit Bats
>
> Fruit bats have long muzzles, large eyes, pointy ears and fury bodies, which is why they are called flying foxes. Unlike Microchiroptera, who travel by echolocation, fruit bats depend on keen vision and sense of smell to navigate. They live in tropical climates that provide them with fruit, flowers and nectar. Some fruit bats as they forage for nectar, are responsible for many types of night blooming trees and plants.

SEQUENCE

- *A text that uses sequence as its organizational structure presents events or steps in chronological order.*

When students are following a sequence of events or chronological pattern they are usually reading or listening to the following types of material:

- historical events
- steps in following directions
- the life of a famous person
- sequence of events in a daily happening
- explanation of a procedure

Chronology 3-D Accordion Book

To aid students in remembering the key information in texts of this kind, they can use a 3-D accordion book. The accordion book can be used to gather information first and then retell, or to retell and transfer this information to notes.

MATERIALS
- 8 ½-by-11-inch sheet of paper
- pencil
- tape or glue stick
- crayons or markers
- oaktag (optional)
- yarn or ribbon (optional)

USING THE STRATEGY

Students can make accordion books any time they want to better remember the sequence of events. There is no one way to fill out the pages of an accordion book. You might ask students to write, or draw, or to do both. It's up to you and the needs and competencies of your students.

To begin, model for students how to make the accordion book. Then, have them follow the instructions below to make their own.

1. Fold the sheet of paper in half lengthwise, and cut it in half so the result is two sheets that are each 4 1/4 by 11 inches.

2. Glue or tape the two sheets together, so the result is one long 4 1/4-by-22-inch sheet.

3. Accordion-fold the sheet five times, to create eight sections or book pages (including front and back cover).

If desired, students can add an illustrated oaktag cover to the front and back of the book. For another way to make these books special, use a hole punch to make a hole on each page along the outside (open) edge. Then string a piece of ribbon or yarn through the holes to tie the book shut.

After reading an article on the processing of maple sugar, fourth-grader Jason made a 3-D accordion book to keep track of all the steps. He used both illustrations and notes. Then he used the accordion book to retell to the class:

> On the cover of my book I drew a picture of a maple leaf because that's the tree we get maple syrup from.

On the second page, I have the farmer putting buckets on the spigots of maple trees in February or March. When the weather changes the sap begins to run.

On the third page, I show the farmer and his family collecting the sap and taking it to the sugar house. Sometimes the sap is taken through plastic pipes to the sugar house.

On the fourth page, you can see the sap being poured into big vats where it will be boiled. You have to boil off all the water. It takes 40 gallons of sap to make one quart of maple syrup.

Jason did a great job using each of the pages of the accordion book to help retell the process of making maple syrup. After he finished, I praised his efforts, and I also gave him something to work toward on his next retelling. I asked him to use transition words next time, instead of saying, "On page one," "On page two," and so on.

Sequence Fact Jar

Students love anything that comes in a special container. There's an air of mystery involved, and they can't wait to see what will transpire. In this activity, students enjoy pulling a slip of paper with a phrase or a picture out of the jar and finding its proper order. However, with the case of fact jar retelling, students not only put themselves in the proper order, they must also retell in detail.

MATERIALS
- jar or canister
- small paper strips

USING THE STRATEGY
Try this activity after students have read a text that involves the sequencing of events. In advance, write the major elements (steps in a process, events in someone's life story, and so on) on slips of paper, and place them in a jar.

1. Invite students to randomly pick slips of paper from the jar. (With first graders, you might wish to draw the elements on the slips of paper rather than write them.)

2. After students have pulled all the slips, ask them to think about the event they have drawn and to prepare to retell about it.

3. Have all the students who have drawn a slip come up and stand in front of the group. Ask each to retell the segment he or she has selected.

4. Ask the class to listen to each retelling segment, and then to decide what order the events came in. Have students arrange the retellers to reflect the proper sequence.

With both of these sequencing activities, students are using visuals and print, and considering main ideas supported by relevant details. The steps involved in a process are not just being read once and tested. Rather, the steps are being reinforced in a number of different methods. Few students can grasp complex information on a first read. The majority of students need multiple run-throughs, which provide a variety of experiences. In providing as many rich and varied experiences as we can, we help our students learn.

Students add their own creative props to the sequencing activity.

CAUSE AND EFFECT

- *When an author is using the cause-and-effect structure, he or she is explaining how some event caused one or more other events to occur. Or, the author may be showing how a particular event or effect is the result of one or more causes.*

Cause-and-Effect Sentence Strips

Cause and effect is a complex textual pattern, but when retelling is aided by graphic organizers, students are able to get a handle on what is actually taking place. In this activity, students identify causes and effects, and write them on sentence strips.

MATERIALS
- sentence strips of different colors
- pencils

USING THE STRATEGY

Pass out to students sentences strips of different colors. Determine which color sentence strips will be used for which category. For example, a blue sentence strip could be used for the cause, red sentence strips for positive effects, and green sentence strips for negative effects. As students complete a reading with a cause-and-effect pattern they should be thinking about or taking notes on the major cause in the story and the related events. Again, the retelling can come before or after the note-taking. After students can identify the major cause(s) and related effects, have them transfer their findings to the appropriately colored sentence strips.

After reading an article on logging in the rain forest, a group of third graders determined the following: *The main cause was cutting down trees in the rain forest for lumber.* Students wrote this on their blue sentence strip.

Then I asked them to think about the good effects of this cutting and to write them on the red strips. I also asked them to think of negative effects and to write those on the green strips.

Later, when it was time for them to retell, I asked for volunteers to share the positive and negative effects from their red and green strips. Encourage students to elaborate, support their statements with clear reasoning, and to incorporate background knowledge whenever possible.

After listening to students retell the positive and negative effects, the other students agreed and disagreed, and I wrote their list on the chalkboard:

Reds: Good Effects

- We have to be able to change. Nothing stays the same in life.

- If the trees are cut for lumber and homes, people will make money.

- Nobody is getting money from the rain forest now.

- When the trees are cut down maybe farming can take place.

Greens: Bad Effects

- The oxygen in the air will be depleted and plants and animals will lose their lives.

- The homes of animals will be lost and they will die. Rare animals will no longer be able to be seen.

- The medicines that come from the rain forest will be lost. People will not get the medications they need.

- The normal balance of nature will be off and more and more problems will take place.

- After all the trees are gone, the land will be barren and nothing will be there. The land will be useless.

Now that the students have read, taken notes, and retold through the use of color-coded sentence strips, they are ready for a discussion of the effects of cutting down trees in a rain forest. They will also soon be ready to put their information in writing if this is the next element in the lesson. A simple essay based on the retelling could follow this format:

- a thesis statement about the topic,

- a paragraph(s) about the positive effects,

- paragraphs about the negative effects and other offshoots, and

- a concluding paragraph about the final analysis.

Of course, this particular piece on the rain forest could also fall into the persuasive comprehension pattern. As students become more sophisticated readers, they will see overlapping patterns. But to readers not at this point, they may still need the color-coded, highly structured sentence strips for retelling and responding.

VARIATIONS

- To make this strategy more suitable for younger children, perform the activity orally, recording the information on a flip chart for students to see.

- To add challenge and complexity to the activity, include further causes based on new effects.

PROBLEM AND SOLUTION

- *A text that relies on the problem-and-solution text structure, presents a problem and then one or more solutions.*

Like cause and effect, the problem-and-solution textual pattern has two parts. And again as in cause and effect, there many be multiple components to the problem and many solutions, some better than others. Additional solutions may come from prior knowledge and some from thinking in creative and novel ways.

Horizontal Flap Book

Horizontal flap books are a terrific prop to help students retell the problem and solutions presented in a text they've read.

MATERIALS

- 8 ½-by-11-inch paper
- scissors
- pencils
- crayons, markers (optional)

USING THE STRATEGY

Have students assemble a flap book following these instructions:

1. Fold 8 ½-by-11-inch sheet of paper in half lengthwise.

2. Unfold the sheet and cut three to five slits, as shown. Cut to within an inch of the fold. Refold at center to create flap book.

3. Along the top of the flap book, beneath the fold, write the problem that is under consideration. Then, on each of the vertical flaps, use a few words to identify different solutions.

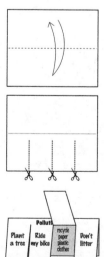

(4.) Lift each flap and write down a few notes that will help you retell each solution in greater detail. (Younger students may use pictures instead.)

Next, you might have students gather in small groups and retell to each other using their flap books. Encourage students to come up with alternate solutions that weren't offered in the text. After everyone has shared, place all of the different retold solutions on the chalkboard. Follow this with a discussion of the pros and cons of each solution.

Finally you can end with a prioritization of the suggestions. After a discussion and prioritization of solutions, you might wish to have students move into a writing activity, a poster, or a mock TV commercial that deals with the problem at hand. The retelling of support information for this and other problems is again getting into persuasive writing. This is a good thing. With this type of pattern modeling, students are beginning to see that when working with authentic materials and strategies everything is not always clear-cut. Everything does not fall, or ever will fall, into a perfect pattern. A good reader is one who can adjust to the reading pattern and content.

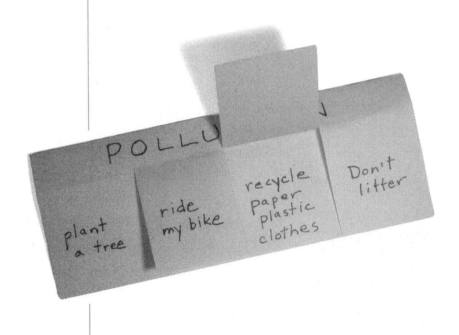

COMPARE AND CONTRAST

- *A text that compares and contrasts shows the likenesses or differences between two or more things or ideas.*

Colored Venn Diagrams

Your students may already be familiar with using Venn diagrams as a visual aid to compare and contrast information. For this retelling activity, we modify the procedure slightly. Instead of two large overlapping circles on a piece of paper, I have students use three colored paper plates attached to craft sticks.

MATERIALS

- paper plates (3 for each Venn diagram)
- craft sticks
- paint or colored construction paper
- scissors
- glue
- pencils
- other craft materials (optional)

USING THE STRATEGY

To compare and contrast two things or ideas, have students work in groups of three.

1. Give each student in the group a paper plate. Instruct two students to paint their plates with one of two different primary colors (see chart below). The third student paints his or her plate with both primary colors, to make a secondary color.

Primary	+	Primary	=	Secondary
Red	+	Blue	=	Purple
Red	+	Yellow	=	Orange
Blue	+	Yellow	=	Green

Note: In place of paint, colored construction paper can be used. In this case, children cover their plates with one of the three colors. For example, one student uses yellow paper, one uses blue paper, and the third uses green paper. Students trace plate-size circles onto the paper, cut them out, and glue them to their plates.

2. Have each student record on his or her colored-paper plate information relating to the elements being compared and contrasted. For example, for a unit on farm animals, you might ask a group of students to compare and contrast cows and horses. (Depending on the age level, students may write or draw these attributes, or represent them in some other way.) The first student records on his or her primary-colored plate things true of cows that are not true of horses. The second student records things true of horses that are not true of cows. The third student, whose plate is colored with a secondary color, will record the areas of overlap—the things that are true of both cows and horses.

3. Once plates are complete, have students attach a craft stick with glue to make a handle.

4. Have each group use their props to orally compare and contrast the items under discussion. They can retell privately to you, to another group, or to the entire class.

The group process at work here adds another dimension and is quite helpful. Instead of being on their own as they read, students are sharing their information, organizing it, and presenting it to others in a pattern-based manner. I find that students don't like to disappoint each other, and that group work often brings out their best effort.

The complementary colored paper plates can be placed in a learning center so that other students can make use of the information in their own research. With this activity, students are learning about color-coded annotation or note-taking as well as the benefits of retelling.

FROM RETELLING TO WRITING

The paper plate props for compare-and-contrast retelling can be taken directly to the writing stage for some students. The student can take information from the red plate and make it paragraph one. Then the student can turn to information on the blue plate for paragraph two. Finally the information from the purple plate, what the two animals have in common, could be the third paragraph. Or students can start with the purple plate information and work backwards. To utilize this information in a five-paragraph essay, students would only need to add an introduction and a conclusion.

PERSUASION (Pros and Cons)

- *In a persuasive text, the author is trying to convince readers to adopt his or her point of view. The writer presents the pros and cons of the issue, but argues that his or her side is the better one.*

Persuasive elements can also be found in many text structures, but some texts are written with this pattern as the organizing principle. Unless students are aware of persuasive techniques and can distinguish fact from opinion, they may be unaware of how they are being manipulated by a particular reading. Persuasive reading and writing certainly involve higher-level thinking skills, but the beginning stages of this form of comprehension can be started in the primary grades.

Seeing Through Different-Colored Lenses

In persuasive texts, writers are trying to convince readers to see things from their point of view. Young readers are often not thinking about a point of view as they read, and they're usually not aware that a piece of writing has a point of view at all. This activity introduces the notion of point of view.

Note that this strategy is best suited to nonfiction passages that deal with topics on which multiple viewpoints are possible, such as logging in the rain forest.

MATERIALS

- eyeglass reproducible (page 82)
- pencils
- scissors
- tape

USING THE STRATEGY

When our students carefully examine a nonfiction passage, we want them to be able to look at the piece through different lenses. Rather than reading it solely through their own eyes, they broaden their understanding when they can shift their perspective and read it through the eyes of someone who is coming from a different point of view. For example, when we looked at the cause-and-effect text pattern (page 72), we looked at how the cutting of trees in the rain forest was affecting humans and the environment. If we looked at the situation through different-colored lenses we could read the story from the point of view of a logger, a village native, a plant or animal that inhabits the village, the logging company president, and so on. Each of these creatures or people has different needs and lifestyles that have an impact upon their view of a particular occurrence.

When students retell through different-colored lenses they put themselves in the shoes of another person or being. They attempt to think outside the box and try to gain another perspective. They learn that there are many facets to any situation.

1. Give students a copy of the eyeglass reproducible on page 82.

2. Explain to students that they will use the reproducible to assist them as they retell the main ideas in the passage from a particular point of view. Tell students that they are to pick someone or something whose point of view that wish to represent. For the topic of logging in the rain forest, they might choose the point of view of a human, an animal, a plant, or anything else that they think might have a viewpoint on the elimination of trees.

3. Have students identify the main issue or problem they are gong to tell about and write at the top of the left and right lens. Then, on the left lens, they are to list the positive aspects of the issue, as seen from their chosen point of view; on the right lens, they are to list the negative aspects from their adopted perspective.

Initially, students use the eyeglasses simply as a graphic organizer. Later, once they've practiced their retelling with the help of this organizer, I encourage them to cut out and assemble the glasses—cutting out the lenses—so that they may put them on, look at the class, and retell from their new perspective.

Retelling for nonfiction forms the same bridge that it does for fiction. The retelling bridge takes students from reading to pattern reinforcement with comprehension. Listening and speaking were our first comprehension skills and we still need to rely on them. And, as with fiction, the ultimate goal of retelling nonfiction is to put students in control or command of what has been read. With retelling, we empower students to take over the roles of reteller, discussion leader, and simulation expert.

Seeing Through Different-Colored Lenses Reproducible

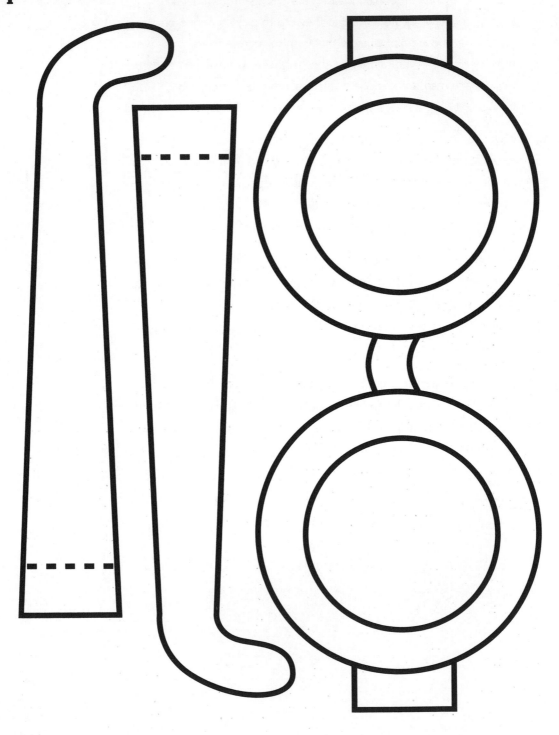

Retelling Extended: Vocabulary Development

As we've seen, retelling is a tool that boosts comprehension skills with fiction and nonfiction texts. In this chapter I am extending the idea of retelling to include vocabulary building. I'll show you how the concept of retelling can be stretched and adapted to become a useful tool to help your students strengthen and enrich their vocabulary.

Using retelling to enhance vocabulary development may seem like a deviation from the comprehension patterns we've been focusing on. It's really not, however. Vocabulary development is an integral part of comprehension, and it's one that is greatly strengthened by retelling and vocalization. When you were a child, did your parents ever quiz you on words for your weekly vocabulary test? If so, hearing your definitions, in your own voice, helped you to remember them for the next day's test.

In using retelling with vocabulary, we aren't simply giving word definitions. We are "working the words" through retelling. If students only see a word, use the dictionary to find a definition, record the information, and take a test, their chances of actually remembering the word or ever using the word meaningfully and naturally are very slim. Instead, vocabulary development that includes retelling encourages students to talk about

- their connections to the word,

- how they are going to remember the meaning,

- people who might need to use the word,

- how they have seen the word in context, and even

- word(s) that might be opposites of the word.

The link between vocabulary and comprehension is clear: a student with a poor vocabulary is never going to be a strong reader. All the retelling props in the world are not going to help if the student does not have a substantial bank of words to draw from. Therefore, we can use retelling strategies and props to help students remember new words just as we do to help boost comprehension.

Word Cubing

The cube is a vocabulary prop that students benefit from greatly. You can make several of these from empty cube-shaped tissue boxes (ask students to bring some in). Cover them with plain paper. Then, have students write and draw on index cards backed with Velcro. Students can make their own cubes using the reproducible on page 87.

MATERIALS

- cube reproducible (page 87; note that you will want to enlarge template)
- crayons or makers
- pencil

and/or:

- premade cubes from tissue boxes
- 3-by-5-inch index cards
- Velcro fasteners

USING THE STRATEGY

A cube has six sides, so this activity asks the student to retell six different word features or associations:

- the word with an illustration
- the word with synonyms
- the word with antonyms
- the word in a sentence
- the word in different forms
- people who might use the word

The student draws or writes one feature on each side of the cube. Here is Cheryl, a fourth grader, using her cube to retell features of the word *grotesque*:

> The word I'm going to talk about is *grotesque*. I drew a picture of the beast from "Beauty and the Beast." Some synonyms for *grotesque* are *distorted*, *outlandish*, and *bizarre*. An antonym for *grotesque* is *beautiful*. People who might use the word would be writers. Different forms of

the word are *grotesqueness*, *grotesquely*, and *grotesquery*. My sentence using the word is, "In 'Beauty and the Beast,' the hunchback is considered grotesque by many people."

As Cheryl talks, she holds her cube and turns it to look at the different sides to help her remember.

After a few retellings, the word and its relationships are very likely to be retained. In fact, after putting this much effort into one word, students' chances of mastery are almost 100 percent.

And where do students learn about other words? They learn about other words through context lessons, content area reading, and listening to the cube retellings by other students. Students even begin to associate certain students with certain words. This type of association can be helpful and provides the necessary link to meaning and usage.

Word Cubing Reproducible

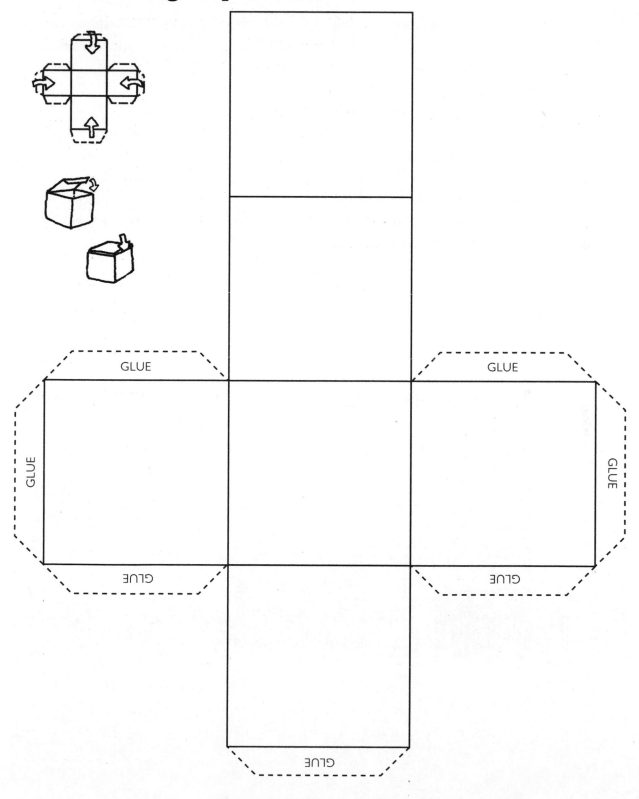

GLUE

GLUE

GLUE

GLUE

GLUE

GLUE

GLUE

Sentence Stripping

Sentence stripping is similar to word cubing (see page 85). Again the chosen word must be looked at from a variety of angles, and the activity culminates in a retelling with a group or the whole class.

MATERIALS

- sentence strips (3-by-24-inch strips of paper or oaktag)
- pencils

USING THE STRATEGY

Students use a sentence strip for each word they will work with. On the strip, they first write the word and then follow with:

- an illustration of the word
- the word's synonyms
- the word's antonyms
- the word in a sentence
- the word in different forms
- people who might use the word

Students use the completed sentence strip as a prop to remember all facets of their new word. Repeated retellings help the word stick.

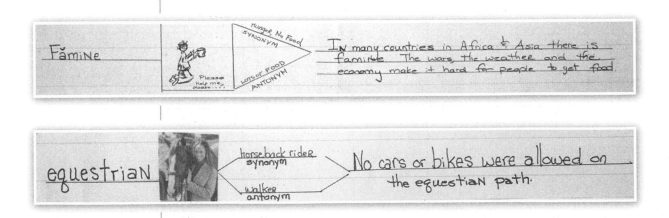

Word Banking

This activity is another variation on Sentence Stripping and Word Cubing. All of these strategies encourage students to look at new words from as many angles as possible. You may already use word banks in your classroom. Have students retell the words in their word banks to gain greater mastery over their chosen words.

MATERIALS

- students' word banks (recipe boxes)
- 3-by-5-inch index cards

USING THE STRATEGY

Have students add words to their word banks, examining the new words from various angles (see Sentence Stripping, page 88). The more ways students look at new vocabulary words, the greater their chance at mastery. Word cards are small and handy, and are perfect for easy study at home or with a partner at school.

In this activity students move fluidly from the definition to the word, and from the word back to the definition. The added element of retelling provides another layer of practice. Remember, retelling props really have a dual purpose. In the beginning, they are used to help students construct meaning; later on, they can be used for study purposes.

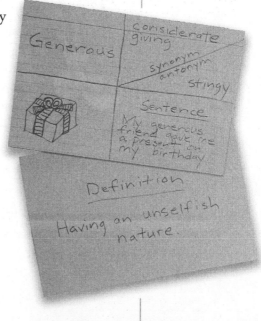

Word Laddering

Teaching students to use context clues is a critical vocabulary-development skill. When students use context to find word meanings, they look both backward and forward in the reading to locate clues that they can link to the unfamiliar word. Students like to think of themselves as being "word detectives" when using context clues.

A word ladder is an easy-to-make prop that lets students work with context clues.

MATERIALS (for each ladder)

- 8 ½-by-11-inch sheet of paper
- pencil
- dictionary

USING THE STRATEGY

To make the word ladder:

1. Have students fold the sheet of paper horizontally in half, then in half for a second time, and in half for a third time. This will produce eight sections.

2. Have students open the paper and refold each section backward and forward, accordion style. The resulting sheet is the word ladder prop.

3. Once students have completed their blank word ladders, the prop is ready to use by filling in each "rung" of the ladder with a possible meaning or synonym for an unknown word. For example, suppose a student encounters the following sentence when reading: *The scientist formed a hypothesis about how the experiment would turn out.* The unfamiliar word here is *hypothesis*. The student looks at the surrounding words in the sentence (and perhaps in other nearby sentences) to come up with possible meanings and then writes them on the ladder rungs. (Often, if a student is working individually, he or she won't complete all eight sections, but may only fill in two or three.)

4. The student now rereads (or retells) the sentence, substituting each possible synonym in place of the unfamiliar word, seeing which new word makes the most sense. As students hear and consider the different words in the sentence they are actively making decisions and assessments.

5. After the student has finished making guesses based on context, he or she looks the word up in the dictionary and writes down the definition.

6. Lastly, the student looks over the word ladder and marks the word or words that best fit the definition.

Keep in mind that sometimes none of the student guesses are correct, and other times more than one is fitting. When you find that a student's guesses are far from the mark, this is an opportunity to provide some guidance or perhaps a mini-lesson on the topic at hand.

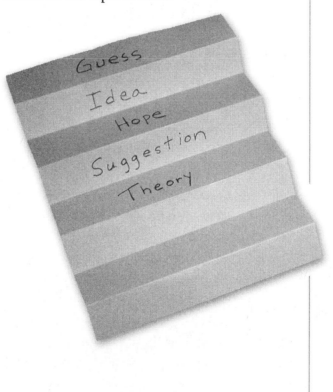

Chunking Flap Book

To uncover new word meanings, experienced readers use the dictionary, context clues, and knowledge of word parts. When students know their word parts or "chunks" and their related meanings, they can predict the meaning of a word even without any context clues. When students "chunk," they break a larger word into smaller parts—often prefixes, suffixes, and root words. This technique allows students to bring prior knowledge to bear when they encounter a word they've never seen before. This process may not always work, but in many cases it will.

MATERIALS

- 8 ½-by-11-inch sheet of paper
- scissors
- pencil
- crayons, markers (optional)

USING THE STRATEGY

To make a chunking flap book, have students follow directions below.

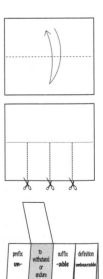

1. Fold 8 ½-by-11-inch sheet of paper in half lengthwise.

2. Unfold the sheet and cut three slits as shown. Do not cut past the center fold. Refold at the center to create flap book.

3. On each of the four flaps, have students write one of the following, in this order: "prefix," "root word," "suffix," "definition."

4. Students will complete the flap book for the particular word they are studying.

   - For example, if the word the student is working with is *unbearable*, on the prefix page, he writes "un." He lifts the flap and on the page underneath he writes "not."

- On the root word page, he writes "bear," and on the flap underneath he writes "to withstand or endure."

- On the suffix page, he writes "able," and on the flap underneath he writes "condition of being."

- On the definition page, the student writes "unbearable," and underneath he writes "not able to be endured."

Of course, every word is not going to fit perfectly into the four-section format. But for teaching about prefixes, roots, suffixes, and common meanings, you can not find a better prop for recording and telling. After students continually hear the same word parts being used over and over in retellings, they get a sense of how knowing word parts or chunks can help when the context is not available or helpful.

Clapping

If a student can not properly pronounce a word, his or her chances of remembering the meaning are very slim. The student will focus on the pronunciation of the word rather than its meaning. To get over this obstacle, we can use the clap-and-retell strategy that is so commonly used with primary-grade students who need help in hearing the number of syllables in a word. This activity helps students master pronunciation along with the word's meaning.

USING THE STRATEGY

Instead of using a graphic organizer or 3-D model for retelling, this strategy uses hands and voices alone. This clapping, in conjunction with the chunked retelling of word parts, can be extremely helpful for students who don't have a strong visual memory and therefore need a lot of auditory and tactile reinforcement.

Here's the basic strategy:

1. Introduce the word. For example, *insurmountable*. Ask students, "How many syllables do you hear?" Clap out the syllables as you say the word. Have students join you in clapping out the word.

2. Ask a volunteer to clap out the word, clapping louder on the stressed syllable and giving a short double clap at the end. Then have the whole class do the same, following the student's lead.

3. Provide students with a definition of the word—for example: "*Insurmountable* means 'incapable of being overcome.' When something is insurmountable, it is very big or very difficult. The story that is going to help me remember the meaning of the word insurmountable is about a group of climbers who attempted to climb Mount Everest but did not make it to the top. Mount Everest is the highest mountain in the world, and for most people climbing to the top is very difficult, if not impossible. In the article I read, some of the insurmountable problems the climbers faced included: the harsh weather, the terrain of the mountain, the condition of the hikers, and not always having the correct equipment. I hope I never run into an insurmountable problem like the ones these climbers faced on Mount Everest. Can anyone tell me about an insurmountable problem in a story you read, a newspaper story, or in your own life?"

Students can keep the clapping going as the retelling continues, if they wish. Students love rhythm and a strong beat. They can easily transfer their musical beat to the beat of syllables and accents. And don't worry about practicing a new word too many times. Students need constant repetition with new words that they need to master.

Retelling with props ups the odds for word recognition, proper usage, and expansion of both spoken and written vocabularies. Our students benefit when we take the time to help them truly understand a word and its various implications. The goal is to allow them to slowly build a bank of words that can be used in speaking and writing. There's no point in teaching words that have no connection or reason for application. On the other hand, words that are relevant to the school curriculum, everyday life, and one's personal life, need to be honored through careful examination and retelling.

Conclusion

In the past, when teachers wanted to check for comprehension they would ask students specific questions. These would often be very literal in nature and required little supportive information or reflection by the student. If students could not answer the question they were told to keep rereading the passage until the answer was found. Now we know that continual rereading without the use of a strategy is often a waste of time.

Structured retelling takes into consideration not only the key information and the specific details of the reading but personal insights and reflections. This retelling also shows the students specifically where they are missing the proper information so that they reread with a particular purpose in mind.

We use the word holistic in education a great deal these days. We want students to look at the whole picture rather than process things in a piecemeal fashion. With retelling, students are working in a global, holistic way so that their learning is meaningful. With retelling strategies students are also self-assessing rather than leaving assessment to the teacher alone. The benefits of retelling are numerous, and I hope you will find a way to bring your students voices more fully your classroom.

References

Professional Books and Articles

Benson, V. (2001). *The Power of Retelling.* DeSoto, Texas: The Wright Group.

Brown, H. and B. Cambourne. (1987). *Read and Retell.* Portsmouth, NH: Heinemann.

Craik, F. M. and Watkins, T.L. (1972). Levels of Processing: A Framework for Memory Research. *Journal of Verbal Learning,* 11.

Dyson, A. H. (1983). The Role of Oral Language in Early Writing Process. *Research in the Teaching of English,* 17.

Fielding, E. N. (1999). *Learning Differences in the Classroom.* Newark, DE: International Reading Association.

Gambrell L. B., Koskinene, P. S., and Kapinus, B. A. (1991). Studies for Retelling as an Instructional Strategy, *Journal of Educational Research,* 84.

Gambrell L. B., Koskinene, P. S., and Kapinus, B. A. (1985). The Effects of Retelling Upon Reading Comprehension and Recall of Text Information. *Journal of Educational Research,* 78 (4).

Gambrell, Linda, Miller, D., King, S., and Thompson, J. Verbal Rehearsal and Reading Comprehension Performance. Paper presented at the National Reading Conference, Austin, Texas, December 1989.

Geist, E. and Boydston, R. (2002). The Effect of Using Written Retelling as a Teaching Strategy on Student Performance. *Journal of Instructional Psychology,* 29 (2).

Gibson, A., Gold, J., and Sgouros, C. (2003). Story Retelling Boosts Children's Reading Comprehension, *Associated Early Care and Education, Associated Child Care and Education,* July/August

Goodman, Y. M. and Watson, D. J. (1988). *Reading Miscue Inventory: Alternative Procedures.* New York: R.C. Owen Publishers.

Hansen, Jill. (2004). Retelling Strategies to Boost Comprehension. *Reading Today,* 21 (6).

Hartman, D. and Allison, J. (1996). Text Talk: Using Discussion to Promote Comprehension of Informational Texts. In Gambrell, L. & Almasi, J.F. (Eds.), *Lively discussions! Fostering engaged reading.* Newark, DE: International Reading Association.

Harwin, S. (1992). *Lasting Impressions: Weaving Literature Into Writer's Workshop.* Portsmouth, NH: Heinemann.

Idol, L and Croll, V. (1981). Story Mapping As a Means of Improving Reading Comprehension. *Learning Disability Quarterly,* 10.

John, V. P. (1970). Story Retelling: A Study of Sequential Speech in Young Children. In Levin, H & Williams, J.P. (Eds.), *Basic Studies on Reading.* New York: Basic Books.

Kapinus, Barbara, Koskinen, P. S., and Gambrell, L. Retelling and the Reading Comprehension of Proficient and Less Proficient Readers. *Journal of Educational Research,* 84 (6).

Labbo, L. & Kuhn, M. R. (2000). Weaving Chains of Affect and Cognition: A Young Child's Understanding of CD-ROM Talking Books. *Journal of Literacy Research,* 32 (2).

Leal, D.J. (1996). Transforming Grand Conversations Into Grand Creations: Using Different Types of Text to Influence Student Discussion. In Gambrell, L. & Almasi, J.F. (Eds.), *Lively discussions! Fostering engaged reading.* Newark, DE: International Reading Association.

Marshall, Norman. (1996). The Students: Who Are They and How Do I Reach Them? In Lapp, D., Flood, J. & Farnan, N. (Eds.), *Content Area Reading and Learning.* Boston: Allyn and Bacon.

Mitchell, J.N. (1983). A Procedure for Assessing the Richness of Retellings. *Journal of Reading,* (26).

Morrow, L. (1985). Retelling Stories: Strategy for Improving Young Children's Comprehension, Concept of Story Structure, and Oral Language Complexity. *The Elementary School Journal,* 75.

Morrow, L. (1986). Effects of Structural Guidance in Story Retelling. *Journal of Reading Behavior,* Vol.18.

Morrow, L. (1986). Effects of Story Retelling on Children's Dictation of Original Stories. *Journal of Reading Behavior,* 18.

Morrow, L. (1985). Retelling Stories: A Strategy for Improving Young Children's Comprehension, Concept of Story Structure, and Oral Language Complexity. *The Elementary School Journal,* 85 (5).

Morrow, L. (1990). *Assessing Children's Understanding of Story Through Their Construction and Reconstruction of Narrative.* Englewood Cliffs, N.J.: Prentice-Hall.

Moss, B. (2004). Teaching Expository Text Structures Through Information Trade Book Retellings. *Reading Teacher,* 57 (8).

Moss, B. (1996). A Qualitative Assessment of First Graders' Retelling of Expository Text. *Reading Research and Instruction,* 37 (1).

Moss, B. Using Retellings to Assess Children's Comprehension of Expository Test. ERIC Document Reproduction Service No. Ed 392 2058.

Murphy, S. (2001). *The Impact of Storytelling and Retelling on Oral Reading and Comprehension.* Phoenix, AZ: Cress Press.

Peach, R. K. and Wong, P. (2004). Integrating the Message Level into Treatment for Agrammatism Using Story Retelling. *Aphasiology,* 18 (5).

Searfoss. K.W. and Readence, J.E. (1994). *Helping Children to Read.* Boston: Allyn and Bacon.

Soundy, C. S. (1993). Let the Story Retelling Begin. *Childhood Education,* 69 (3).

Taylor, B. (2000). The Effects of Text Structure Instruction on Middle Grade Students' Comprehension and Production of Expository Text. *Reading Research Quarterly,* 19.

Wells, G. (1986). *The Meaning Makers: Children Learning Language and Using Language to Learn.* Portsmouth, NH: Heinemann.

Whaley, J. (1981). Story Grammars and Reading Instruction. *Reading Teacher,* 34.

Wixson, K. K. (1986). Vocabulary Instruction and Children: Comprehension of Basal Stories. *Reading Research Quarterly.*

Children's Books

Appelebaum, D. 1993. *Giants in the Land.* Boston: Houghton Mifflin.

Allard, H. G. 1985. *Miss Nelson Is Missing.* Boston: Houghton Mifflin.

Amstel, M. 2000. *Sybil Ludington's Midnight Ride.* Minneapolis, MN: Carolrhoda.

Barrett, J. 1982. *Cloudy With a Chance of Meatballs.* New York: Aladdin.

Berends, P. 1998. *I Heard Said the Bird.* New York: Puffin Books.

Brett, J. 1999. *Gingerbread Baby.* New York: Putnam.

Brett, J. 1996. *The Mitten.* New York: Putnam.